Bernes

Daniel Anker

Bernese Oberland East

Translated by Gill Round

50 selected walks in the valleys and mountains around Interlaken –
Lauterbrunnen – Grindelwald – Meiringen

With 72 colour photos, 47 small walking maps to a scale of
1:500,000, 1:100,000, 1:125,000
and an overview map to a scale of
1:450,000

ROTHER · MUNICH

Cover Foto:
The highest peak of the Bernese Alps, with the Finsteraarhorn (4273m) as
your companion: hiking near the Lauteraarhütte (Walk 36).

Frontispiece (page 2):
The path along the Grimselstausee goes through the protected
Arvenwald in the direction of the Lauteraarhütte (Walk 36).

All photos by Daniel Anker, except those on pages 83 (Walter Anker)
and 92 (Emanuel Balsiger).

Cartography:
Small walking maps to a scale of 1:50,000, 1:100,000
and 1:125,000 © Bergverlag Rother (drawn by Ingenieurbüro Heidi
Schmalfuß, Munich). Overview maps to a scale of 1:450,000 and
1:600,000 © Freytag & Berndt, Vienna.

Translation: Gill Round

1st edition 2004
© Bergverlag Rother GmbH, Munich

ISBN 3-7633-4827-1

Distributed in Great Britain by Cordee, 3ª De Montfort Street, Leicester
Great Britain LE1 7HD, www.cordee.co.uk
in USA by AlpenBooks, 3616 South Road, C-1, Mukilteo, WA 98275 USA,
www.alpenbooks.com

ROTHER WALKING GUIDES

Algarve · Andalusia South · Azores · Bernese Oberland East · Corsica · Côte d'Azur ·
Crete East · Crete West · Cyprus · Gomera · Gran Canaria · Iceland · La Palma · Madeira · Mallorca ·
Mont Blanc · Norway South · Provence · Pyrenees 1, 2, 3 · Sardinia · Sicily · High Tatra · Tenerife ·
Tuscany North · Valais East · Valais West · Vanoise · Around the Zugspitze

**Dear mountain lovers! We would be happy to hear your opinion
and suggestions for amendment to this Rother walking guide.**

BERGVERLAG ROTHER · Munich
D-85521 Ottobrunn · Haidgraben 3 · Tel. (089) 608669-0, Fax -69
Internet www.rother.de · **E-mail** bergverlag@rother.de

Foreword

'Neither Chamonix nor Zermatt, in my opinion, is equal in grandeur and originality of design to the Bernese Oberland. No earthly object that I have seen approaches in grandeur the stupendous mountain wall whose battlements overhang in mid-air the villages of Lauterbrunnen and Grindelwald; the lower hills that rise beneath it, like the long Atlantic rollers beaten back from the granite cliffs on our western coast, are a most effective contrast to its stern magnificence; in the whole Alps there is no ice-stream to be compared to the noble Aletsch glacier, sweeping in one majestic curve from the crest of the ridge down to the forests of the Rhone valley; no mountains, not even the aiguilles of Mont Blanc, or the Matterhorn itself, can show a more graceful outline then the Eiger – that monster, as we may fancy, in the act of bounding from the earth.' The Englishman Leslie Stephen (1832-1904), the first ascentionist of large peaks like the Schreckhorn (in 1861), Bietschhorn, Zinalrothorn or Monte Disgrazia, not only shaped the history of alpinism, but, with the appearance in 1871 of the book 'The Playground of Europe' also determined exactly how the Alps have been perceived in the last 250 years: the playground of Europe.

The Bernese Oberland, especially its eastern part with the central points Lauterbrunnen and Grindelwald, is considered to be the birthplace of alpine tourism. It was here that the poets discovered the beauty of the mountains. The Alps was the brief and succinct title that the Bernese Albrecht von Haller gave to his pioneering poem in 1732 which was read by poets and lesser mortals who, as tourists, followed in the footsteps of Haller and Stephen at first by carriage and boat, then later by train and car. The German born, later Swiss nationalised, Johann Gottfried Ebel maintained in his book, first published in 1793 and translated into English in 1818 'The traveller's guide through Switzerland' that there is no more healthy exercise, more strengthening or life-enhancing, than going on foot through mountain country.

Let us experience the world at the bottom of the Eiger, Jungfrau and Schreckhorn on foot. This Bernese Oberland East guide book is intended as a 'small pocket book', just like Jakob Samuel Wyttenbach's book from the year 1777, to 'show the stranger the right way'.

Bern, summer 2004   Daniel Anker

Contents

Tourist tips

Grades: from really easy to very demanding

Most of the walks described here in the eastern part of the Bernese Oberland (and the bordering regions in the Valais) go along marked paths. In the pre-alpine and alpine country, however, there are times when sure-footedness and a lack of vertigo are essential. The length and variation in height of many of the walks require an appropriate amount of fitness. Route finding might also be necessary sometimes, even on marked routes. In order to give you an idea of the grade of each walk at a glance, the route numbers are printed in different colours as follows:

BLUE

These paths are well marked, usually comfortably broad, hardly exposed and only moderately steep. They do not require any previous mountain experience and can usually be undertaken with relatively little danger in bad weather. These walks rarely take longer than 4 hours. 11 of the walks in this guide are marked blue, but depending on the chosen route, can also change to red in places!

RED

These mountain paths are adequately marked, but sometimes narrow and exposed. There are certain sections which have been made safe. Some sure-footedness and fitness are required and also a lack of vertigo, and suitable equipment (e.g. good footwear) is absolutely necessary. The walking time on these walks can be as much as 8 hours. 31 of the walks in this guide belong to the red category.

BLACK

These paths – sometimes marked (perhaps even as official hiking paths), but sometimes not – are really only suitable for sure-footed, fit and experienced mountain walkers with a good head for heights. You might even have to use your hands over some steep and rocky ground. There are no walks across glaciers, but sometimes you need to cross over old snow fields and here walking sticks have proved to be useful. 8 walks in this guide are classified as black.

Train, bus and boat: public transport to the start and from the end of your walk

All locations, starting points and destinations of the 50 walks described in the eastern Bernese Oberland are easily accessible by public transport. There's a dense network of trains, buses and boats. The relative details from Switzerland's official guide to transport regarding train lines, bus numbers, connections and timetables for each walk are given in the square brackets. Three numbers = train, 3+2 numbers = buses (of private companies) and postautos (yellow, Swiss State buses), 4 numbers = cable railway, boat. The telephone numbers for buses and cable railways are also in the transport guide where further information is available. The guide consists of two volumes: blue = trains, cable railways, boats; yellow = buses. Regional timetables are handy and you will find very useful: www.rail.ch.You can also call timetables up on your mobile (as long as there is a signal): www.rail.ch/pv/sms_e.htm.

Chästeilet: joining in the folk festivals

Where cheeses are cut in autumn and where strong men try to flatten each other in the sawdust ring (this Swiss national sport is called 'Schwingen'), where shepherds' festivals take place and whatever else there is to do as a change from hiking, all this information can be found in the local tourist office.

Give the car a miss – you don't need one for a hiking holiday around the Eiger or in the Oberland.

Length of time: up to the nearest ¼ hour

The walking times are based on a walking speed of about 4km an hour under normal conditions over level ground or up to about 300m on an incline. Stops are not included. The walking times are rounded up to 15 minutes so there's a difference from the time details given on the signposts.

Getting there

How do you get to the Bernese Oberland? By train, of course, whether you land in Zürich-Kloten or in Geneva. There are trains that go direct to Interlaken; sometimes you can also change trains in Bern, the capital of Switzerland. If, on the other hand, you land in the small airport of Bern-Belpmoos, take the bus to Belp station from where a train goes every 30 minues to Thun. If you want to travel the whole way by train: depart London Waterloo at 12.04, arrive Paris-Nord at 15.59, depart Paris Gare de Lyon at 16.44, arrive Bern at 21.24, depart Bern at 21.30, arrive Interlaken West at 22.26; if the changeover time is too short, take an earlier Eurostar. Interlaken is also a destination for international trains: the EuroCity from and to Hamburg is

Eastern path into the Oberland – old Susten road with Steingletscher (Walk 41).

simply called the Bernese Oberland. More info about trains and timetables at www.rail.ch.

Guidebooks: load up your rucksack

- Loretta and Philip Alspach: *Bernese Oberland – A travel guide with specific trips to the mountains, lakes and villages*, Intercon Pub, 2001.
- Marcia and Philip Lieberman: *Walking Switzerland – The Swiss Way: From Vacation Apartments, Hotels, Mountain Inns and Huts*, The Mountaineers, 1987.
- Clem Lindenmayer: *Walking in Switzerland*, Lonely Planet, 2001.
- Kev Reynolds: *The Bernese Alps – A walking guide*, Cicerone Press, 2001.
- Kev Reynolds: *Alpine Pass Route Switzerland*, Cicerone Press, 2001.
- Les Swindin: *Bernese Oberland*, Alpine Club Guide Books, 2003.
- Jean and Philip Talboys: *Easy Ways to the Plants of the Bernese Oberland*, Sawd Publications 1993.

■ Marion and Maurice Teal: *Bernese Oberland: Thirty Circular Walks from Regional Centres*, Pathmaster Guides 2001.

Use of the guide: a network of day walks

The contents page gives you an overview of the walks described in the guide and is divided into five regions; there's a short introduction to each of these regions. The walks have been chosen so that the destination of one walk coincides with the start of the next. There's a tight-knit network of paths with all the necessary tourist information throughout the whole of the eastern Bernese Oberland between the Brienzer Rothorn and Grimselpass, Interlaken and Sustenpass.

The most important information for each individual walk is given in fact-file form: location, starting point and destination, walking times and height variation, grade and season, food and accommodation, interesting places to visit, map, variations to the walk, linking walks and useful tips. The description of the route follows a characterization of the walk. The line of the route is drawn on a section of map. A photo completes the description. Overview maps show you the geographical location of all the walks, and all the mountains, passes, destinations, locations, starting points and bases are contained in the index at the back of the book.

Height variation: even the descent should be noted

Ascent and descents are given since stamina is not only required for walking uphill, but also (perhaps even more) for putting on the brakes to go downhill. The height details are taken from the national map of Switzerland and the decimetres are only given at important points.

Information: tourist office addresses

General: www.MySwitzerland.com; www.berneroberland.com.

■ Alpen Region, Brienz-Meiringen-Hasliberg, 6084 Hasliberg, ☎ 033 972 51 51, fax 033 972 50 55

■ Brienz Tourism, 3855 Brienz, ☎ 033 972 80 80, fax 033 972 50 55

■ Engelberg-Titlis Tourism, Tourist Centre, 6390 Engelberg, ☎ 041 639 77 77, fax 041 639 77 66

■ Goms Tourism, 3984 Fiesch, ☎ 027 970 10 70, fax 027 970 10 75

■ Grindelwald Tourism, 3818 Grindelwald, ☎ 033 854 12 12, fax 033 854 12 10

■ Interlaken Tourism, Höheweg 37, 3800 Interlaken, ☎ 033 826 53 00, fax 033 826 53 75

■ Kiental Tourist Office, 3723 Kiental, ☎ 033 676 10 10

■ Langnau Tourism, Dorfmühle 22, 3550 Langnau im Emmental, ☎ 034 409 95 95, fax 034 409 95 98

■ Lauterbrunnen Tourism, Bahnhofplatz, 3822 Lauterbrunnen, ☎ 033 856 85 68, fax 033 856 85 69

■ Meiringen-Haslital Tourist Information, 3860 Meiringen, ✆ 033 972 50 50, fax 033 972 50 55
■ Melchsee-Frutt/Kerns Tourism, 6064 Kerns, ✆ 041 660 70 70, fax 041 660 71 75
■ Mürren Tourism, 3825 Mürren, ✆ 033 856 86 86, fax 033 856 86 96T
■ Thunersee Tourism, Postfach, 3602 Thun, ✆ 033 251 00 00, fax 033 251 00 88
■ Wengen Tourist Information, 3823 Wengen, ✆ 033 855 14 14, fax 033 855 30 60

Try www.rother.de (WebLinks/GeoSuche) for many useful links.

Season: summer sun on the Jungfraujoch

A good time for hiking in the Bernese Oberland is the summer, from July to the beginning of October. In June and from the middle of October you should take account of old and new snow in the higher areas, while the lower destinations are accessible throughout late spring and autumn. If you are hiking in the autumn you must take note of the running times of the mountain railways and post buses as well as the possible military shooting practices.

When the Föhn (name of a strong warm wind) is blowing you should avoid walks along the main ridge of the Bernese Alps, for example, on the Grimselpass. On the other hand, in the lower part of the Föhn valleys, it can be sunny (and windy). The Swiss weather report is updated five times a day: you can access it by telephoning (✆ 162) and listening to the radio; at 12.20 on Radio DRS1 there's a very comprehensive report; the reports are shorter at 7.30 and 16.50. Furthermore Meteo Swiss publishes daily from 17.00 the local weather report in English (✆ 157 126 211 or 0900 55 21 11) as well as the weather report for the Alps (✆ 157 126 218 or 0900 55 21 38). There's personal weather advice on ✆ 900 16 23 33. Also very useful: www.meteoswiss.ch and www.meteomedia.ch. Weather forecasts and reports can also be accessed on your mobile with the SMS news flash (details: www.meteoswiss.ch).

Maps: many walking maps

The maps refer to the national map of Switzerland of swisstopo: 4 numbers = scale 1:25,000; 3 numbers = scale 1:50,000. If there's a 'T' with it, then the map is also available as the official walking map of the 'Schweizer Wanderwege' (Swiss hiking paths). Map 2520 'Jungfrau Region – Unesco World Natural Heritage' to a scale of 1:25,000 is also very good. You will find many other maps with walking routes marked on them which are often annotated and they are usually published by the local tourist offices based on the official national map. The following can be recommended:

A sight to quicken the pulse – summit book and map.

- Jungfrau-Region, Oberhasli (Bernese Oberland Ost), 1:60,000, Kümmerly+Frey (covers all the walks in this guide with the exception of the ascent from Engelberg to Trüebsee – works well as an overview).
- Grindelwald, 1:25,000, MPA publishers and tourist office
- Grimsel-Furka-Susten, 1:50,000, Naturfreunde Schweiz (Switzerland for nature lovers), MPA publishers
- Lauterbrunnen–Mürren–Wengen, 1:40,000, Lauterbrunnen Tourism
- Kiental–Griesalp–Reichenbach, 1:25,000, Egger publishers, Frutigen

Literature: From Byron to Doyle
- Daniel Anker: *Eiger – The Vertical Arena*, The Mountaineers 2000.
- George Gorden Byron: *Manfred, a dramatic poem*, 1817.
- Alphonse Daudet: *Tartarin on the Alps*, Routledge 1887.
- Arthur Conan Doyle: *The Final Problem,* 1893.
- Bob Langley: *Traverse of the Gods*, Michael Joseph 1980.
- Leslie Stephen: *The Playground of Europe*, Longmans, Green 1871.
- Paul Townend: *The Man on the End of the Rope*, Collins 1960.
- Mark Twain: *A Tramp Abroad*, 1880.
- Trevanian: *Eiger Sanction*, Heinemann 1973.

Military: they shoot with live ammunition
It's possible that in the Bernese Oberland, and sometimes also in the neighbouring central area of Switzerland, that the military carry out shooting practices on weekdays (except in high summer) in various places like, for example, the Urbachtal and in Eriz. So when the notes on 'season' refer to this

particular danger, it is recommended that you check beforehand with the regional information office about military shooting: Bern (✆ 031 324 25 25). If you come across abandoned shells in shooting areas, do not attempt to touch them, just note their location and report them (✆ 117).

Protection of nature and the environment
- ■ Do not pollute the environment with your exhaust fumes or your litter.
- ■ Protect all animals, plants and rocks (minerals).
- ■ Show respect for the locals and their property (alpine meadow huts, animals); close field gates after you.
- ■ Stay on marked paths.

Route finding: left is not just on the left
The details left/right are according to whether you are making an ascent or a descent; however, on the right-hand side of the valley, on the right-hand bank are expressions based on the direction of flow of the water. The names are given according to the national map of Switzerland to a scale of 1:25,000. Features of the local landscape have on the whole been left in their local form.

A favourite sport – mountain hiking, below the Wetterhörner (Walk 28).

Pass: Swiss or regional
The various branches of the Swiss tourist office (Schweiz Tourismus) will have more information if you want to use a Swiss-Pass, Swiss-Flexi-Pass or Swiss-Card when travelling (www.MySwitzerland.com):
- ■ *Australia and New Zealand*
  Walshes World Agencies Pty. Ltd., GSA Swiss Air Lines, Lvl 3, 117 York, AU-Sydney, NSW 2000, Australia.
- ■ *Benelux*
  - Postbus 75387, NL-1070 AJ Amsterdam, Netherlands.
  - Suisse Tourisme, Boîte postale 1600, BE-1000 Bruxelles, Belgium.
- ■ *Great Britain and Ireland*
  Swiss Centre, 10 Wardour Street, GB-London W1D 6QF, Great Britain.

■ *Japan*
  Toranomon Daini Waiko Bldg. 3F, 5-2-6, Toranonmon, Minato-ku, JP-Tokyo 105-0001, Japan.
■ *Nordic Countries*
  c/o Embassy of Switzerland, Birger Jarlsgatan 64, SE-10041 Stockholm, Sweden.
■ *North America*
  - Swiss Center, 608 Fifth Ave, US-New York, NY 10020, USA.
  - 926 The East Mall, CA-Toronto, Ontario M9B 6K1, Canada.
  - 501 Santa Monica Blvd., Suite 607, US-Santa Monica, CA 90401, USA.

Also recommended: Bernese Oberland regional pass for 7 or 15 days, with 3 or 5 days free travel on many of the (mountain) railways and with 4 or 10 days 50 % reduction. Bookable online: www.regiopass-berneroberland.ch.

Rescue: inportant telephone numbers
■ Swiss air rescue REGA ℡ 1414
■ Police ℡ 117
■ Ambulance ℡ 144

Sport: varied program
Sport is the major pastime in the playground of Europe. In alphabetical order: alpinism, badminton, travelling by hot air balloon, canyoning, curling, hang gliding, fishing, paragliding, golf, cross country skiing, high mountain walking, hydro speed, inline skating, climbing, running, mountain biking, horse riding, river -rafting, sledging, rowing, swimming, lake kayaking, sailing, skiing, snowboarding, diving, tennis, windsurfing – and hiking, of course.

Trekking: the most beautiful multi-day walks
47 of the 50 walks described in the guide are day walks; many of them can be joined together to make multi-day walks. Three beautiful treks are:
■ Round the Brienzersee: blue above and below, and in between, white scree slopes, green meadows and ridges. Stay overnight up on the mountains if possible to enjoy the sunrises and sunsets.
  The stages: 1. Interlaken-Schynige Platte; 2. Schynige Platte-Faulhorn; 3. Faulhorn-Giessbach-Brienzer Rothorn; 4. Brienzer Rothorn-Bitschigrind-Oberried; 5. Oberried-Augstmatthorn-Harder-Interlaken. See Walks 23, 24, 26, 2, 4, 5.
■ Peaks around the Jungfrau: seven days, seven summits (if you include the Tanzbödeli as one of them), three nights in the tourist villages of Mürren, Wengen and Grindelwald, three nights in huts and mountain hotels with magnificent views, and always with the Jungfrau, the highest and most brilliant peak of the Oberland trio, in the focal point, but from

The beautiful Jungfrau (4158m) – where you can spend a week trekking around its base.

different perspectives. In short, an unforgettable week of walking in the Jungfrau region.

The stages: 1. Saxeten – Bällehöchst – Suls – Lobhornhütte; 2. Lobhornhütte – Soustal – Bietenhorn – Mürren; 3. Mürren – Gimmelwald – Busenalp – Tanzbödeli – Obersteinberg; 4. Obersteinberg – Stechelberg – Trümmelbachfälle – Wengen; 5. Männlichen – Kleine Scheidegg – Grindelwald; 6. Grindelwald – Reeti – Faulhorn; 7. Faulhorn – Schynige Platte – Geiss – Wilderswil. See Walks 9, 11, 14, 15, 18-20, 27, 24, 23.

■ Oberhasli walk for experienced hikers: if you want to do this walk along the most breathtaking mountain paths you will need to be as fearless and untiring as Sherlock Holmes. There are chasms lurking in many places, for example, near the Reichenbach fall, which was the great detective's undoing.

The stages: 1. Meiringen – Reichenbachfall – Rosenlaui; 2. Rosenlaui – Dossenhütte; 3. Dossenhütte – Innertkirchen; 4. Innertkirchen – Bänzlauialp – Furtwangsattel – Windegghütten; 5. Windegghütten – Furen – Tällihütte; 6. Tällihütte – Klettersteig Tälli – Engstlenalp; 7. Engstlenalp – Melchsee – Hochstollen – Käserstatt – Hasliberg. See Walks 32, 31, 38, 39, 42, 47.

Accommodation: huts and hotels
Where possible, individual telephone numbers are given for suggested accommodation, together with opening times, number of beds and other important information. For accommodation in the area you should contact the tourist offices or access www.berneroberland-hotels.ch. In most of the accommodation you will be able to get a meal, but the same doesn't always apply in reverse.

Provisions: milk and alpine cheese
You can buy provisions in all villages in the Oberland, and even on Sundays in the larger tourist resorts. It is also possible to buy food on the walk itself on occasions: a piece of cheese, for example, in a staffed alpine hut or from a mountain farm and there's usually a sign advertising direct sale from the meadows. You can also buy cheese, milk and sometimes coffee with cream in the mountain restaurants on the way.

Paths: yellow, white/red/white and white/blue/white
The waymarking of the hiking trails and mountain paths in Switzerland and in the principality of Liechtenstein is consistent and made in accordance with the guidelines drawn up by the Schweizer Wanderwege (Swiss hiking paths). The waymarkings consist of signposts with or without time details, directional arrows, rhomboids and colour markings. Walking routes are waymarked yellow and the most demanding mountain routes, white/red/white. Even more difficult are the unofficial alpine routes and they are waymarked white/blue/white. The Berner Wanderwege organisation (Bernese hiking paths) has constructed and waymarked in the canton of Bern a network of paths which total a good 9,000km in length, with more than 1,200 different routes and over 10,000 signposts.

Aim: another 50 Oberland hikes
Further information about the Bernese Oberland and more importantly, 50 other walks which sometimes link up seamlessly with those in this guide, can be found in the Rother walking guide *Bernese Oberland West: Thunersee – Gstaad – Lenk – Kandersteg*' (available as German or French edition).

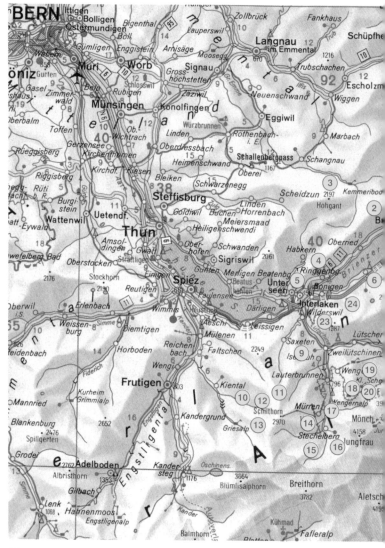

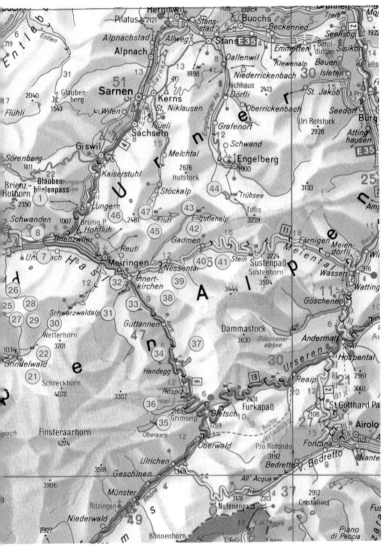

Brienzersee: mountains and boats

'Its shores are surrounded by stately, high, forest-covered mountains and jagged rocks', was noted to the Brienzersee in 1844 in the first Baedeker travel guide in Switzerland; published into English in 1864 under the title *'Switzerland. Handbook for travellers'*, thus getting into competition with John Murray's well established *'A handbook for travellers in Switzerland and the Alps of Savoy and Piemont'*, 1st edition in 1838. With the headword 'Brienz' the Baedeker states 'How strange and melodic is the song of the ferrywomen, almost all of them pretty, who row visitors across the lake.' Tourism in the Bernese Oberland has been fuelled by these contrasting elements of splendour and the bucolic since its beginnings. The 'belles batelières de Brienz' sometimes awoke more than romantic feelings in the male travellers at the start of the 19th century. The annulled marriage between a nobleman from Neuenburg and the ferrywoman Elisabeth Grossmann was staged in Paris.

Even without rowing boats, a boat ride across the Brienzersee makes an enjoyable end to a walk (Walks 6, 26). On the other hand, if you would like to meet the locals and see their work, you should visit the Ballenberg open-air museum at Brienz (Walk 8). Some of the activities include more than 20 handicraft skills on display by experts who are working according to traditional methods: from baking to cheeses, bobbin lace and basket making to weaving. About ten of the crafts and trades are on view every day. Ballenberg has between 250,000 and 300,000 visitors every year. So that visitors to the site cannot become completely immersed in this fascinating past, military jets from the neighbouring aerodrome in Unterbach can be heard roaring overhead in spring and autumn. The Ballenberg open-air museum allows you an informative and, at the same time, enjoyable day's journey on foot through a Switzerland that no longer exists.

Past and present: if you stop at the Weisses Kreuz hotel built in 1688 you will see pictures of Goethe, Uhland and Byron on the wall. Like so many others, these poets came down here because Brienz lay on the standard tourist route in the Bernese Oberland which leads from Interlaken via Lauterbrunnen, Grindelwald and Meiringen and across the intervening Kleine and Grosse Scheidegg (Walks 20, 30) to Brienzersee. Lord Byron, who promoted Switzerland in England with his drama *'Manfred'*, published in 1817, the location of which was the Wengernalp, (like Schiller with his *'William Tell'* in Germany) wrote in his diary on 24th September 1816: 'Four Swiss country girls came from Oberhasli in the evening and sang songs from their area; two of the voices were beautiful – the melody too; they also sing in this Tyrolean manner.' The next morning the journey continued from Brienz to Interlaken: 'Out on the Brienzter lake in a long rowing boat which was rowed by women (one very young and very pretty – I sat down beside

Brienz harbour where visitors used to be rowed across the lake by women.

her and began to row).' The English traveller noticed later on: 'Ate lunch in Interlachen. Girl gave me a few flowers and spoke to me in German, which I do not understand at all: I don't know if the words were pretty, but the girl was.'

Today in the busy streets of Interlaken you can also hear many women's English and American voices. And as you stroll along, if you look up above the souvenir shops and palatial hotels, you will see the stony face of the Hardermandli on the Harder in a favourable light (Walk 5). According to legend the face belongs to Prior Leonhardus from Interlaken monastery who took advantage of a beautiful fisherman's daughter from Ringgenberg on the Brienzersee and was banished to eternal damnation onto these rocks on the mountain behind the Oberland tourist centre.

1 Arnihaaggen, 2207m – Brienzer Rothorn, 2349m

Ideal approach to the (eastern) Bernese Oberland

Brünigpass – Wilervorsess – Gibel – Arnihaaggen – Brienzer Rothorn

Starting point: Brünigpass (1002m) on the trainline [470] Interlaken-Luzern.
Destination: Brienzer Rothorn (2349m); compare Walk 2. Information Rothorn train: ✆ 033 952 22 22.
Walking times: Brünig – Wilervorsess 1½ hrs., Wilervorsess – Gibel 2 hrs., Gibel – Arnihaaggen 45 mins., Arnihaaggen – Brienzer Rothorn 1½ hrs.; total time 5¾ hrs.
Difference in height: ascent 1530m, descent 180m.
Grade: need for absolute sure-footedness. The marked path is exposed in places and might be awkward in the autumn due to ice in shady spots.
Best season: June to October.
Eating places and accommodation: Ho-

tel Brünig-Kulm (✆ 033 971 17 08). Hotel Brünig (✆ 033 971 11 33). Naturfreundehaus Brünig (✆ 041 678 12 33). Hotel Rothorn Kulm (✆ 033 951 12 21).
Things to look out for: a quite spectacular path with wonderful views.
Map: 244 T Escholzmatt, 255 T Sustenpass; 1189 Sörenberg, 1209 Brienz.
Alternatives: the direct route via Chäseren instead of Arnihaaggen is less exciting and not much shorter. From Schönbüel (2011m), inn and Lungern mountain station of the cable railway on the Brünig line, in 2½ hrs. onto the Rothorn; summiters with a head for heights will also want to walk over the Höch Gumme (2205m).
Linking walks: 2, 46.

'The highest point of the mountain chain of the Brienzer ridge is the Rothorn, famous for its view which is only just second to that from the Faulhorn. Since it has a good restaurant up on top, better than the one on the Faulhorn, it is visited more often than the Faulhorn', – so we read in the first edition of Baedeker's *Die Schweiz – Handbüchlein für Reisende'* (Switzerland. Handbook

Breathtaking views down to the Brienzersee – western ridge path at Arnihaaggen.

for travellers) from 1844. It was not possible to check which of the mountain hotels is better today, but the view from the Brienzer Rothorn, and also from the Arnihaaggen, is still just as good: the view goes from Sustenhorn to Diablerets and from Jurabogen across Säntis back to Dammastock – breathtaking just like the views down into the valley from this much-used path where passing and overtaking is not always easy due to its precipitous nature.

From the station on the **Brünigpass** go along the road in the direction of Meiringen as far as the restaurant on the bend. The ascent begins here on the right. On a forestry road, always taking the left-hand turn-offs, climb up through the wood. A short, scrubby path leads up to the forest clearances of Totzweg. Go north to **Wilervorsess** (about 1400m), where the narrow hiking path starts which leads across the precipitous, grassy south side cut by crumbling gullies out onto a ledge. Just afterwards in Salewang, take the right-hand path which crosses up onto the **Tüfengrat** col (1858m). Along Scheidegg ridge, only a step's width in one place, ascend onto the shoulder of **Gibel** (2040m) where the hiking path joins from Schönbüel. The path blasted out of the sometimes vertical south side of Höch Gumme leads over to the adjoining ridge onto **Arnihaaggen** and reaches its southern summit round a few zigzag bends; the north summit is five metres higher. Descend from Arnihaaggen along the western ridge and on an exposed path on its north side onto **Eisee col** (2025m). Go steeply up to the trig point and to the viewing terrace of the **Brienzer Rothorn**.

2 Ällgäu Lücke, 1918m

From the highest peak of the canton of Luzern through the Oberland into the Emmental

Brienzer Rothorn – Planalp – Bitschigrind – Ällgäu Lücke – Kemmeriboden

Location: Brienz (566m); on the train line [470] Interlaken-Brünig-Luzern. Or Sörenberg (1162m); post bus [460.60] from Schüpfheim on the line [460] Luzern- Bern.

Starting point: Brienzer Rothorn (2348m); cog railway [475] from Brienz or cable car [2505] from Sörenberg.

Destination: Kemmeriboden Bad (976m); compare Walk 3.

Walking times: Brienzer Rothorn – Planalp 2 hrs., Planalp – Bitschigrind 2 hrs., Bitschigrind – Ällgäu Lücke 30 mins., Ällgäu Lücke – Kemmeriboden 2 hrs.; total time 6½ hrs.

Difference in height: ascent 650m, descent 2000m.

Grade: only for surefooted hikers; narrow path only a shoe's width and slightly overgrown on unstable grassy slope between Salibiel and Bitschigrind. Marked paths.

Best season: June to October.

Eating places: Planalp restaurant.

Accommodation: Brienzer Rothorn; compare Walk 1. Hotels in Brienz and Sörenberg. Hotel Kemmeriboden Bad (✆ 034 4937777). Gasthof Alpenrose in Bumbach (✆ 034 493 31 33). A shepherds' hut is situated on Bitschigrind, mostly open, with straw bunks, wood and stove.

Things to look out for: the white 'meringues' in Kemmeriboden Bad.

Map: 244 T Escholzmatt, 254 T Interlaken; 1189 Sörenberg, 1209 Brienz.

Alternatives: from Brienzer Rothorn by train to Planalp (1341m); also on foot from Brienz via Gäldried (2½ hrs.). From Oberried station on the Brienzersee in a good 3 hrs. Directly up to Bitschigrind. Summiters can climb from Ällgäu Lücke in 15 mins. along the exposed ridge path onto Chli Schnierenhörnli (about 2040m; no height or name given on the map; summit book). Descent across the grassy north hillside and below the summit rocks on the right back to the hiking path.

Linking walks: 1, 3, 4.

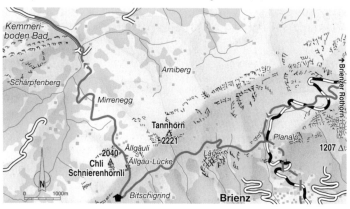

The cog railway has been puffing onto the Brienzer Rothorn above the Planalp since 1892.

'The journey with this unique steam cog railway onto the 2350m high mountain is a once in a lifetime experience and affords especially good views.' So promises the Brienzer Rothorn railway leaflet. It was constructed from the Luzern side using a cable car. Due to the trains and the very popular hike in the direction of Brünigpass (see Walk 1) there's almost the same hustle and bustle on the highest point of the Luzern canton as on the lakeside promenade of its capital. If you want to experience the Brienzersee and the high white Alps on the horizon on your own, you should choose the walk over Ällgäu Lücke.

From the summit of **Brienzer Rothorn** go past the mountain station (about 2290m) of the cable car from Sörenberg back to **Hotel Kulm** (2266m). You can get here also from the mountain station (2244m) of the cog railway. The hiking path to **Planalp** goes across the steep grassy hillside out onto the crest of the ridge where a breathtaking view opens up down the hillside. Continue across the southwest hillside to Oberstafel and over a steep ledge to Greegsi, then along the hiking path and a little alpine meadow road to Planalp (1341m). Just above this on the right turn onto the little road that leads towards Läger (1698m). Go along the very narrow ridge path in places across the precipitous south-eastern flank of the Brienzer ridge via Salibiel onto **Bitschigrind** (1690m). A beautiful alpine connecting path leads across the steep hillside up onto **Ällgäu Lücke**. Gently descend the north side, past the alpine settlement of Ällgäuli and go along a moorland path to Mirrenegg (1383m). Descend the tarmac road to the Emme. Follow the left bank to **Kemmeriboden Bad**.

3 Hohgant, 2196m

Summit walk over the northern bastion of the Oberland

Kemmeriboden Bad – Furggengütsch – Vordere Hohgant – (Aff) – Hohgant West – Trogenhorn – Innereriz

Starting point: Kemmeriboden Bad (976m), postbus [line 460.50] from Wiggen on the trainline Bern-Langnau-Luzern [460].
Destination: Innereriz-Säge (1040m), terminus for the bus from Thun [300.60].
Walking times: Kemmeriboden – Furggengütsch 4½ hrs., Furggengütsch – Vordere Hohgant 30 mins., Vordere Hohgant – Hohgant West 1 hr., Hohgant West – Trogenhorn 45 mins., Trogenhorn – Eriz 1¾ hrs.; total time 8½ hrs.
Difference in height: ascent 1500m, descent 1440m.
Grade: fitness and sure-footedness needed; unmarked paths in places.
Best season: June to October. Sometimes shooting practice in the autumn on the north side of the Trogenhorn.
Eating places and accommodation: Landgasthof Kemmeriboden Bad; compare Walk 2. Blockhütte Hohgant, no name on the map, private self-catering hut of the Emmental branch of the SAC, 25 places, locked hut, info and key, ℂ 034 402 51 11. Innereriz: Schneehas (closed Mond./Tuesd. ℂ 033 453 18 38);   Säge (closed Wednesdays ℂ 033 453 13 21).
Things to look out for: the numerous cairns on Furggengütsch (looks like a site of pagan worship). The nicely constructed zig-zag path across the northwest side and gully of Trogenhorn.
Map: 244 T Escholzmatt, 254 T Interlaken; 1189 Sörenberg, 1208 Beatenberg, 1209 Brienz.
Alternatives: without Furggengütsch and Trogenhorn 1¼ hrs. shorter. Even Hohgant West can be circumnavigated.
Linking walk: 2.

East to west traverse of the whole massif which protrudes into the hilly Emmental area, often narrow paths, only short stretches on little roads, four summits, an extra peak, a thrilling 360° panorama – in brief, this is what lies in store for you on a ridge walk in the heart of the Swiss nature reserve of Hohgant.

From **Kemmeriboden Bad** go up the valley along the little road to the junction on the Harzisboden. Continue along the right-hand roadway to **Schärpfenberg** (1271m) and the hiking path to the **Blockhütte Hohgant**

The summit of Furggengütsch is the highest point in the Hohgant nature reserve.

(1805m). Going north-westwards along the marked path into the funnel between the pre-summit of (Vordere) Hohgant and Furggengütsch, and then go up towards a col and along the west ridge, a little bit exposed, to **Furggengütsch** (2196m), the highest point of the Hohgant massif. Return into the afore-mentioned funnel, but steep at first, then on the level onto the summit roof of the actual Hohgant which is called **Vordere Hohgant** (2163m) for easier identification. Cross the stony and grassy summit plateau without paths in a westerly direction; the unmarked path begins where it narrows to the ridge. This leads on the south side around the ridge tower of the **Aff** (2036m); you can also go over the top (more difficult; two short exposed places where you will have to use your hands). The path follows the Wysschrüzgrat onto a first and a second col (1976m) and now runs on the level far below the ridge into a basin. In order to climb up to Hohgant West, leave it a few minutes after the place where you descended a short way over a rocky step. Some tracks across a steep grassy slope ascend on the left of a slab and over the topmost section of the east ridge onto **Hohgant West** (2070m). A little bit further southwest at Point 2063m there's a summit cross and a book. From here go on a marked path along the south ridge onto the Chrinde col (1968m) and along the west ridge onto Trogenhorn col (1870m, not named on the map); ladders make the descent easier through a steep gully; the path is exposed in places. Go over the east ridge onto **Trogenhorn** (1973m); in the middle section there's a steep step with a ladder and at the top, some huge boulders. Continue on the path along the southwest ridge onto a col. The path zigzags down through the northwest gully and the steep hillside into the depths below; finally go over to the Hof **Obere Breitwang**. Go along an access road as far as the crossroads at the hostel and on the hiking path directly along a ridge down to **Innereriz-Säge.**

4 Augstmatthorn, 2137m

Ridge walk with unique views in the foreground and into the distance

(Interlaken) – Harder – Horet – Suggiturm – Augstmatthorn – Schwend-allmi – Habkern

Location: Interlaken (567m); east station.
Starting point: Harder Kulm (1322m); compare Walk 5.
Destination: Habkern (1068m); postbus [line 300.90] to Interlaken West.
Walking times: Harder Kulm – Horet 1¾ hrs., Horet – Augstmatthorn 1¾ hrs., Augstmatthorn – Schwendallmi 1¾ hrs., Schwendallmi – Habkern 1 hr.; total time 6¼ hrs.
Difference in height: ascent 850m, descent 1100m.
Grade: long mountain walk which demands absolute sure-footedness. Marked, sometimes exposed paths.
Best season: end of May to October.
Eating places: Harder Kulm.
Accommodation: in Interlaken; compare Walk 5. In Habkern Hotel Bären (✆ 033 843

11 82); Sporthotel (✆ 033 843 13 43). Naturfreundehaus Schwendi (1175m) in the hamlet of Tschieme east of Habkern; 35 places (✆ 033 843 12 02 and 843 13 81).
Things to look out for: the flowers (in June) close up, the ibex close up and the Jungfrau a bit further away.
Map: 254 T Interlaken; 1208 Beatenberg, 1209 Brienz.
Alternatives: from Oberried (589m) on the Brienzersee and on the train line [470] Interlaken-Luzern, zigzagging up onto the Blasenhubel (1965m) and along at times very narrow north eastern ridge onto the Augstmatthorn; 1650m ascent, 6 hrs., mostly marked path but exposed in the upper section; lack of vertigo is needed.
Linking walks: 2, 5.

Where ibex look at the Jungfrau (on the right) – summit ridge on the Augstmatthorn.

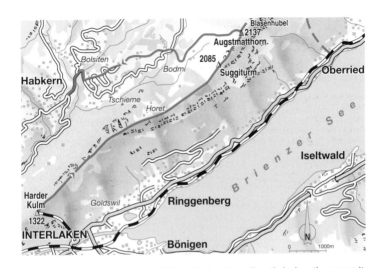

Way down below, just under 1600 vertical metres directly below the summit, the blue-green Brienzersee and the huge peaks of the Bernese Alps opposite: the view from the Augstmatthorn has it all. And if you are at all interested in animals, this ridge walk will certainly give you your money's worth.

Harder Kulm, reached in only a few minutes from the mountain station of the cable railway, is where the almost never ending southwest ridge begins onto Augstmatthorn. The mountain path leads through the wood and clearings, on the ridge itself or on its southern side, going round the ridge elevations of Wannichnubel (1585m) and Roteflue (1730m), continuing onto the alpine pastures of **Horet**. Continue along the now mostly sunny mountain path along the ridge or a little on the left of it. The ridge swings steeply up to **Suggiturm** (2085m; Suggiture on the map), a peak which is often confused with Augstmatthorn. A rather laborious path relieves the ascent. From Suggiturm go along a really exposed, but good path over to **Augstmatthorn**. From the summit return a short way back along the south western ridge, then go westwards across precipitous grassy slopes and a rocky steep step onto a ledge. go on southwards over a rib to the alpine huts of **Bodmi** and along a little road to the Lombach and to the road which comes down from the Rotenschwand pass. Keep going along this to the next hairpin bend, then westwards along the hiking trail to **Schwendallmi** (1405m). Carry on down across meadows wherever possible on the hiking path and not on the little access roads. You reach the road at the bottom and follow this over the Bolsiten bridge (1041m) to **Habkern-Post**.

5 Harder Kulm, 1322m

The most beautiful viewpoint above the Oberland tourist centre

Interlaken Ost – Hardermandli – Harder Kulm – Unterseen – Interlaken West

Starting point: Interlaken (567m), east station, intersection of the lines to Bern [310], Luzern [470] and onto the Jungfraujoch [311/312].

Destination: Interlaken, west station on the line [310] to Thun-Bern.

Walking times: ascent 2½ hrs., descent 2 hrs.; total time 4½ hrs.

Difference in height: ascent and descent, both 750m.

Grade: short, steep walk on well-marked paths; sure-footedness necessary for the

descent route.

Best season: April/May to October/November; also in winter if there's no snow on the ground. In the cold season you should pay extra special care to the frozen paths in places.

Eating places: on Harder Kulm.

Accommodation: in Interlaken, from the Grand Hotel Victoria-Jungfrau to Balmer's Herberge (✆ 033 822 19 61).

Things to look out for: the mixed woodland with beech trees, larch, spruce and holly. The game preserve with ibex and marmots at the valley station. The Harder Kulm mountain hut. The townscape of Unterseen. Interlaken by night.

Map: 254 T Interlaken; 1208 Beatenberg.

Alternatives: by the funicular, opened in 1908 (8 mins.); runs from the beginning of May to the end of October. From Harder continue onto Augstmatthorn; compare Walk 4.

Linking walks: 4.

Tip: Tell open-air theatre (June to September). Unspunnenfest, since 1805 the tradition-packed folklore festival in Switzerland (there have been eight up to now with the next one in 2005). Mystery Park.

In the Pavillon Hohbüel you can see who else has been there: Felix Mendelssohn-Bartholdy, Richard Wagner, Carl Maria von Weber. From Harder Kulm you have the best view of Interlaken lying between the lakes and surrounded by enormous mountains some of which this guide introduces in more detail.

From **Interlaken East** station go westwards towards and across the Aare bridge. The footpath starts immediately on the left of the Harderbahn valley station. Wind your way uphill and go along a little road left to the Pavillon Hohbüel. The path zigzags steeply up through a beech wood, crosses a small road several times and after going under the rails of the funicular, reaches the larch grove of Obere Bleike. Continue diagonally upwards, again under the funicular, to the picnic area (1113m) on the top of **Hardermandli**. The path goes back towards the railway lines, runs out to Hardermatte and climbs along the ridge to the sun terrace and mountain hut of **Harder Kulm**. Return to Hardermatte, but this time take the really narrow path to **Unterseen** which leads round long drawn out bends downhill through a steep wood. At the edge of the wood at the bottom go left, past the cemetery, then to the right and to Unterseen. Walk beside the Aare or through the little medieval town of Unterseen itself and you eventually arrive directly by **Interlaken West** train station.

View through the larches – Interlaken in the autumn light.

6   Shoreline path along the Brienzersee

To the Grand Hotel and the waterfalls of Giessbach

(Interlaken) – Iseltwald – Giessbach Falls – (Brienz)

Starting point: Iseltwald (566m); bus [300.86] or boat [3470, from middle April to end October] from Interlaken East.
Destination: Giessbach (566m); boat connection to Brienz on the train line Interlaken-Luzern [470]; or via Iseltwald back to Interlaken.
Walking times: Iseltwald – Giessbach boat quay 1½ hrs., ascent to the hotel and circular walk to the falls about 1 hr.; total time 2½ hrs.
Difference in height: ascent and descent, both about 150m.
Grade: a stroll, but along a surprisingly stony path.
Best season: spring to autumn; some icy sections in winter.
Eating places and accommodation: various hotels in Iseltwald. Grand Hotel Giessbach (May to Oct . ✆ 033 952 25 25).
Things to look out for: Iseltwald village, boat quay and Grand Hotel Giessbach, the funicular in between (the first mountain railway in the Oberland, 1879).

Map: 254 T Interlaken; 1209 Brienz.
Alternative: on foot from Giessbach to Brienz (but it's not worth the effort).
Linking walks: 7, 26.
Tip: for 200 years Brienz has been famous for its wooden carvings. In the 'Swiss Wood-carving Shops' you can buy bears, alpine horns, dolls in traditional costume, all carved in wood. You can also pay a visit to a canton wood-carving school and two wood-carving workshops.

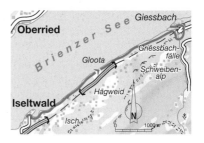

The idyllic shoreline path opened in 1977 from **Iseltwald** to Giessbach had to be built because of the construction of the motorway further up the hillside. The Giessbach Grand Hotel built in 1875/76, once the most elegant address in the Oberland, had to be demolished, but is magnificent in its newly-found glory today. Then there's also the roar of the 14 waterfalls of the Giessbach.

Walk along **Iseltwald** harbour bay to the shoreline path. The path which is hewn out of the rock in places leads through the wood, as close as possible to the Brienzersee, to Giessbach; in Gloota half way along there's a picnic area with fire rings. In Giessbach, before the building for the cable railway and boat quay, turn off right and ascend towards the Grand Hotel but turn off right below, before you reach it and at the next opportunity cross over the Giessbach again. Go left at the following crossroads and along a protected, gorse-sprayed path below a waterfall. Descend the right-hand shoreline and go along the little road to the **Grand Hotel Giessbach**. Leisurely descend the right-hand broad path after that down to the boat quay.

A good idea to combine a walk to the Giessbach Falls with a boat trip.

7 Hinterburgseeli, 1514m

On the shady side of the Oberland: planes, roadways and nice resting places

Axalp ob Brienz – Hinterburgseeli – Uf der Flue – Züün – Meiringen

Location: Brienz (566m); trainline Inter-laken- Meiringen-Luzern [470].

Starting point: Axalp (Kurhaus, 1535m); bus [470.95] from Brienz.

Destination: Meiringen (595m).

Walking times: Axalp – Hinterburgseeli 45 mins., Hinterburgseeli – Uf der Flue 45 mins., Uf der Flue – Meiringen 2½ hrs.; to-tal time 4 hrs.

Difference in height: ascent 230m, de-scent 1170m.

Grade: easy mountain walk which merely requires some fitness and staying power along tarmac (meadow) roads on the de-scent to Meiringen.

Best season: May to November; the lake is normally frozen over from November to May.

Eating places and accommodation: Sporthotel in Axalp with bunk house (℃ 033 951 16 71). Hotels and youth hos-tel in Meiringen.

Things to look out for: the alpine pas-tures with acorn trees on the descent to Züün, birthplace of Melchior Anderegg, the 'king of mountain guides'.

Map: 254 T Interlaken; 1209 Brienz, 1210 Innertkirchen.

Alternative: from Uf der Flue across the northern precipices of Oltschiburg and Axalphorn back onto Axalp (graded red).

Linking walks: 6, 30, 32, 45.

Tip: also possible by mountainbike; but you reach Hinterburgseeli along the al-pine meadow road which branches off on the bend at Point 1185m of the Axalp road.

This is not a spectacular walk – there are more splendid mountain lakes, hik-ing paths and viewpoints – and yet this is a Bernese Oberland against the grain, lacking the usual Jungfrau, Schreckhorn and Wetterhorn on the hori-zon, but with a mountain lake that has an underground outflow and is sur-rounded by steep walls (established as a nature reserve) and an amazing view down to Brienz and the low Meiringen plain instead. The airfield has a presentiment of evil. In fact, during the week, military jets usually set off from here to bombard the Axalphorn. The mountains are not only used by moun-tain people and tourists.

From **Axalp** health resort go eastwards along the path via Schlagli and the Gausband (about 1640m) to the **Hinterburgseeli**. For a short way follow a

The deep Hinterburgseeli where picnics are not forbidden.

path along the north shore, over a hilltop onto a roadway and to the right. The hiking trail shortens the bends of the meadow access road on the ascent to Hinterburg, but eventually joins it. It runs over viewpoint Point 1645m to the alpine huts of **Uf der Flue** (1548m). Now continue along the former beautiful alpine path across meadows and through clearings to Wirzen (1247m).

Go along the little road through the scattered settlement of **Züün** (means fence), until after the Säge when the old path turns off and leads below the road over the steep step down to the valley floor. Walk along a field path across the plain to the Balm crossroads. Cross the Aare and the plain again to **Meiringen** station.

8   Ballenberg open-air museum

A stroll through Switzerland's country architecture and way of life

Brienz – Ballenberg – Brienzwiler

Starting point: with the Brünig train [470] from Interlaken or from Luzern to Brienz (566m). Shuttle bus of all trains from Brienz station to the west entrance of the open-air museum. 10 minute walk from Brienzwiler train station (between Brienz and Meiringen) brings you directly into the 'Tessin'. From May to September there's a free shuttle service in the afternoon between the east and the west entrance.

Walking time: 1 hr. to 1 day.
Difference in height: negligible.
Grade: no special requirements.
Best season: the open-air museum is open from mid-April to 31. October daily from 10.00 to 17.00.
Eating places: four restaurants in the open-air museum, as well as picnic areas and barbecues. Food and drink can also be bought there.
Accommodation: in Brienz, Brienzwiler and Hofstetten.
Things to look out for: there are many open-air museums, but this one in Ballenberg is a must.
Map: 254 T Interlaken; 1209 Brienz.
Tip: combined tickets and special offers from all Swiss railway stations. Daily program of the open-air museum and other information from ℂ 033 952 10 30 or 952 10 40; www.ballenberg.ch.

Lively open-air museum – spindle makers as an added attraction.

Idyllic scene below the Brienzer Rothorn: rescued buildings of the Bernese Mittelland.

The Swiss open-air museum for country architecture and living on the Ballenberg near Brienz has been in existence since 1978. On the piece of ground which is 6 hectares in size, stand 100 historic buildings from all over the country. All the buildings were in danger of being demolished in their original location and could not be preserved; instead of tearing them down they were rebuilt on the Ballenberg and gently restored in order to preserve for posterity certain relics from former times. The museum buildings have been equipped with the appropriate furnishings and fittings and surrounded by historic country gardens, meadows and fields where they cultivate long-forgotten or extinct grasses and types of grain, and tend ancient breeds of pets.

There's no need for a walk description. Whichever route you decide to take round the museum is interesting and each group of buildings is well worth seeing. It's easy to find your way around the hilly site where the buildings are grouped in hollows according to the different regions of Switzerland. Information boards provide you with an overview and an excellent short guide can be purchased very cheaply from the kiosks at the entrance.

Lauterbrunnen valley: water and walls

Another mountain here its steep rock face lifts,
A stream from wooded heights goes plunging to its fall;
The foaming river's jet is forced through jagged rifts
And with unfettered strength shoots far beyond its wall.

This is Albrecht von Haller's description of Staubbach waterfall in the Lauterbrunnental from his didactic poem published in 1732, 'The Alps', a key work for those with a general alpine enthusiasm and for Bernese Oberland tourists in particular. In his 490 verses, the Bernese polymath praises the wild beauty of the mountains and the beautiful freedom of its inhabitants. Thanks to the advertising by poets and painters, travel writers and travel companies, the classic U-shaped valley carved out by glaciers, into which plunge 72 waterfalls, has become the dream holiday destination for city-dwellers who are tired of civilisation. The Trümmelbach Fälle (Walk 17) which thunder down within the rock faces, impart just the same awesome feelings which travellers in Goethe's time were seeking.

'One of the most terrifying and dramatic regions of our part of the earth' was how the alpine explorer Gottlieb Sigmund Gruner described in his book 'Die Eisgebirge' des Schweizerlandes in 1760 (The ice mountains of Switzerland) the furthermost part of the Lauterbrunnental. Othmar Gurtner saw it differently in his book 'Schlechtwetterfahrten' (Journeys for Bad Weather) in 1917: 'I can think of nothing more beautiful than a late summer's evening in the Steinberg. There the tired sun playfully shines onto the glistening hanging glacier which way above is free of snow, and the Rottal glows like a ruby in the sun's fire. Add to that the black cone of shade in the twilight-lit valley and a cheeky yodel wafting over from a goatherd on the Schafberg – there is nothing nicer in the whole world!' Dreadful or beautiful – both judgements on the nature reserve of the Hinteres Lauterbrunnental are right in their own way, as you will ascertain on your trips to the Obersteinberg (Walk 15) or to Busenalp (Walk 14), the venue for the one-time erotic bestseller, Mimil.

The Jungfrau either as the beautiful Alpine dairymaid or the 4158m high peak: hardly any other peak, conquered in 1811 by silk factory workers and chamois hunters (although not from the unfriendly Lauterbrunnen side, but across the tame Aletsch glacier), has kindled the traveller's desire to write. The professor of philosophy from Göttingen, Christoph Meiners, thought in 1785: 'I do not think that there is a more noble and, at the same time, more beautiful mountain than the Jungfrau in the whole world.' You come very close to the Jungfrau if you climb up to the Rottalhütte (Walk 16) or from Wengen over the Biglenalp to the Eiger glacier (Walk 18).

If you have ever seen the TV broadcast of the annual Lauberhorn downhill skiing race, you will never forget the pictures of the amazingly daring skiers sweeping down the slopes in front of the face of the Jungfrau. However the

Extremely beautiful – the Hinteres Lauterbrunnental with the Grosshorn, Breithorn and Tschingelhorn.

first resort for the Alpine downhill ski sport is not Wengen, but Mürren which also lies on a terrace high above the valley. It was here in the 20s that ground-breaking Englishmen, amongst others Sir Arnold Lunn, invented downhill skiing and the slalom.

However, when you are hiking there's no need for you to cover an area as quickly as you can. It's appropriate therefore that Mürren and Wengen are car-free resorts. The Lauterbrunnental has always been the cradle of tourism and probably always will be and from 13.12.2001, its furthermost region has belonged to the Jungfrau-Aletsch-Bietsch-horn area in Unescos' World Natural Heritage.

9   Bällehöchst, 2095m – Sulegg, 2412m

A rather tiring walk onto two neglected viewpoints

Saxeten – Underberg – Bällehöchst – Sulegg – Suls-Lobhornhütte – Isenfluh – Zweilütschinen

Starting point: Saxeten (1103m); post bus [Linie 311.10; reservations recommended] from Wilderswil on the line [311] Interlaken East – Zweilütschinen – Lauterbrunnen.

Destination: Isenfluh (1081m), with bus connection [311.20] to Lauterbrunnen; Zweilütschinen (652m). Possible too from Sulwald (about 1520m) by cable car [2458] to Isenfluh (daily service).

Walking times: Saxeten – Bällehöchst 3¼ hrs.; Bällehöchst – Sulegg 1¾ hrs., Sulegg – Lobhornhütte 1 hr., hut – Isenfluh 1½ hrs., Isenfluh – Zweilütschinen 1 hr. total time 8½ hrs.

Difference in height: ascent and descent, both 1400m. Another good 400m more descent to Zweilütschinen.

Grade/requirements: fitness and sure-footedness essential; marked paths except the one onto Sulegg (only feint tracks, but still easy).

Best season: July to September.

Accommodation: hotels in Saxeten, Iseltwald and Zweilütschinen/Gündlischwand. Suls-Lobhornhütte, private hut of the SAC Lauterbrunnen branch, open and staffed from June to middle of October; booking recommended from Familie Feuz, Lischmaad, 3822 Lauterbrunnen (℡ 079 656 53 20 or 033 855 27 12).

Things to look out for: summits, paths and a hut. The old church path from Isenfluh to Zweilütschinen is an object of national importance. Map: 254 T Interlaken; 1228 Lauterbrunnen.

Alternatives: without detour onto Bällehöchst and Sulegg (about 2 hrs. and 500 vertical metres less). From Suls along the high mountain trail to Sousläger and as in Walk 11 to Grütschalp (1486m).

Linking walks: 10, 23.

'Amongst the many unknown viewpoints incomprehensibly left behind on Helvetia's mountains, Suleck is one of those which deserves more attention than is normally devoted to it, due to its special location and its diverse and dramatic views along the admittedly rather tiring path; however swarms of travellers, unaware of the nearby ridges, waltz along the beaten track in the valley at the foot of the rocks and only see piece by piece what can be experienced up here in a whole panorama', Conrad Escher stated in his contri-

The last steps onto Sulegg – view of Brienzersee and Schynige Platte.

bution '*Kleine Bergreise auf die Sul oder Suleck. Donnerstag, den 18. Juli 1806*' (Short mountain journey onto Sul or Suleck. Thursday, 18. July 1806) for the magazine 'Alpina'. Since then nothing has changed.

From **Saxeten** go up the valley along a little road to **Underberg** (1457m). Descend the valley along a marked path to the alpine huts of Hinder and Usser Bällen (1882m). Go up onto the col (1998m) between Sulegg and **Bällehöchst** (2095m) onto the top of which it's worth making a short detour. At the foot of the northeast wall of Sulegg cross the precipitous slopes of Tschingel (dangerous if there's still snow about!) onto a shoulder (about 2040m) below Schärihubel (2124m). Keeping right along some tracks go up onto it and along the broad grassy south-eastern ridge onto the summit also called **Höji Sulegg**. From the top return along the ascent route to the marked path. In a roughly southern direction go along a little path to the Suls-Lobhornhütte (1955m) – or to Sulsseewli as well – and down onto **Alp Suls** (1903m). The hiking path leads mostly through forest, close to the sunny meadows of Sulwald, and crossing an alpine road several times, brings you down to **Isenfluh**. Just below the valley station of the Sulwald cable car, in spite of the new road, there's a well-preserved church path – previously Isenfluh's only connection to the outside world – down into the Lauterbrunnen valley. Finally go along the road out of the valley and across the Weisse Lütschine to **Zweilütschinen** station.

10 Schwalmere, 2777m

Summit covered in scree with brilliant views

Lauterbrunnental – Soustal – Schwalmere – Spiggegrund – Kiental

Starting point: Grütschalp (1486m) above Lauterbrunnen; compare Walk 11.
Destination: Kiental village (958m) or Griesalp (1408m); compare Walk 13.
Walking times: Grütschalp – Soustal 1 hr., Soustal – Schwalmere 4½ hrs., Schwalmere – Spiggegrund 3 hrs., Spiggegrund – Kiental 1 hr., Spiggegrund – Griesalp 2 hrs.; total time about 10 hrs.
Difference in height: ascent 1420m, descent 1940m; 500m more ascent on the path to Griesalp.
Grade/requirements: strenuous walk which demands route finding and good visibility; if it's foggy, it's difficult to follow the mostly marked, but sometimes un-

clear paths over the stony ground.
Best season: July to September.
Accommodation: hotels to be found in Lauterbrunnen. Suls-Lobhornhütte; compare Walk 9. Kiental; compare Walk 12. Griesalp: Gasthaus Golderli (✆ 033 676 21 92).
Things to look out for: the Oberland from high up.
Map: 254 T Interlaken, 264 T Jungfrau; 1228 Lauterbrunnen, 1248 Mürren.
Alternatives: from Isenfluh, Sulwald or Suls-Lobhornhütte via Suls up onto Sousegg. The Klein Lobhorn (2518m) along the easy western ridge.
Linking walks: 9, 11, 12, 13.

What a long weekend! The Lobhornhütte on Friday (Walk 9), over Schwalmere and Abendberg on Saturday onto Griesalp, Gspaltenhornhütte and

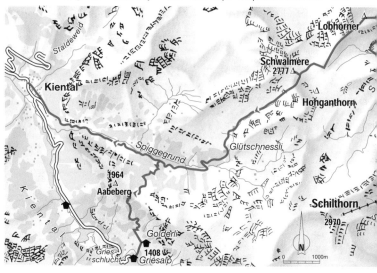

View from Sulegg – Schwalmere lies just to the right of the snowy col.

Sefinenfurgge on Sunday to Mürren (Walk 13). If you still have time on Monday you can stay overnight in the Rotstockhütte and get to the Hinteres Lauterbrunnental via Schneeige Lücke – Tanzbödeli (Walk 14).

From **Grütschalp** follow Walk 11 to Sousläger; short descent to the valley bottom (about 1650m). On the level go up the valley along the **Sousbach** as far as the confluence of the Chantbach. Climb up beside this and go diagonally over the Sousböden onto Sousegg (2150m). Now go along the ridge over Schwarze Schopf to the Lobhörner, across its southern faces onto a ridge (about 2490m) and down onto a col (2372m). A track covered in scree leads south-westwards onto the Schwalmere col (2674m); in early summer or autumn there are usually snowfields. Walk leisurely along the ridge onto **Schwalmere**, then return to the Schwalmere col. The path descends diagonally across the precipitous, stony and grassy southern hillside and leaves it over a ledge (at Point 2074m). Go down onto Glütsch meadow (1940m). Below Glütsch rocks the path leads to **Glütschnessli** (1638m). Take the roadway into the Spiggegrund and continue along the little road down the valley as far as the turn-off (1387m) to Aabeberg. Either continue through the **Spiggegrund** as in Walk 12 to **Kiental** or go over Schwand and Mittelberg into the (1885m) **Chanzel** notch east of Aabeberg and down to the **Golderli** mountain inn and **Griesalp**.

11 Bietenhorn, 2756m

A little visited pyramid almost vertically above the Lauterbrunnen valley

(Lauterbrunnen) – Grütschalp – Soustal – Bietenlücke – Schilthornhütte – Allmendhubel – Mürren

Location: Lauterbrunnen (795m); train [line 311] from Interlaken East.
Starting point: Grütschalp (1486m), transfer station for the train [313] Lauterbrunnen-Mürren.
Destination: Mürren (1638m). Allmendhubel funicular [2463] runs from June to October.
Walking times: Grütschalp – Sous-Oberberg 2 hrs., Oberberg – Bietenhorn 2½ hrs., summit – Schilthornhütte 1 hr., hut – Mürren 1½ hrs.; total time 7 hrs.
Difference in height: ascent 1270m, descent 1120m; only 850m in descent if you use the Allmendhubel funicular.
Grade/requirements: really strenuous walk for sure-footed mountain walkers with a head for heights. Mostly wallmarked paths, protected in places. Slightly exposed summit ridge. Be careful of the old snow in early summer (north side of the Bietenlücke).
Best season: July to October.
Eating places: Allmendhubel. Sonnenberg and Suppenalp restaurants in the Blumental, on the indirect descent from Allmendhubel to Mürren.
Accommodation: hotels in Lauterbrunnen and Mürren. Sous-Oberberg alpine meadow hut (2000m), Matten ski club, 15 places, key and information: ✆ 033 823 05 82. Schilthornhütte, Mürren ski club, 40 places, open and staffed from beginning of July to the end of September, ✆ 033 855 50 53 or 079 656 82 00.
Things to look out for: natural scree

slope (as in the descent from the Bietenlücke) as opposed to the ski slope scree deposited by the digger.
Map: 254 T Interlaken, 264 T Jungfrau; 1228 Lauterbrunnen, 1248 Mürren.
Alternative: from Lauterbrunnen on foot to Grütschalp; 2 hrs. Northface-Trail from Allmendhubel to Mürren with twelve information boards; brochure available.
Linking walks: 10, 12, 13.
Tip: leaflet on '*Baukultur Mürren entdecken*' (discovering the architecture of Mürren).

The wonderful panorama from the Bietenhorn of the Eiger, Mönch and Jungfrau is just one highlight of this walk. Together with views out from the summit, you are also afforded views inwards of the wounds that winter sports leave behind between the Lauterbrunnental and the Soustal. Hopefully you will think about this when you descend in winter from the Schilthorn past the Bietenhorn to Mürren.

Go horizontally at first from **Grütschalp**, then later gently ascend in a northerly and then westerly direction through forest to the alpine huts of Sousläger at the start of the **Soustal**. Continue along the orographical right-hand side of the valley, past the alpine huts of **Oberberg** (2000m) and make your way to the end of the valley. Turn sharp left onto the Schlächti Matti and go out of the valley below the rock faces of the Schwarzgrates diagonally across scree up into the Bietenlücke (2639m). Go left and on tracks along the at first narrow, then later on broader southwest ridge to the summit of **Bietenhorn** where you need to scramble left in a narrow cleft in the rock over a step at the beginning of the ridge. Return from the summit also called Schwarzbirg, into the Bietenlücke and continue a short way along the ridge. Now descend left being careful over the slippery terrain; finally keep right to the **Schilthornhütte** (2432m). Go eastwards along a broad path down to the **Kanonenrohr**. The route below this splits into two: either go along the ridge to the **Allmendhubel** (1907m) where you can take the funicular, or go on foot along the south side of the Hubel to **Mürren**.

Discovered on the other side of the valley – house in Wengen (in December).

12 Schilthorn, 2970m

Hero's walk onto the overdeveloped, highest peak of the Bernese pre-Alps

Kiental – Spiggegrund – Glütschnessli – Hohkien – Rote Härd – Schilthorn – (Mürren)

Starting point: Kiental village (958m); compare Walk 13.

Destination: Schilthorn (2970m); 4 sections of cable car via Birg (2677m), Mürren (1638 M), Gimmelwald (1363m) to the valley station (862m); post bus [311.15] to Lauterbrunnen; train [311] to Interlaken. Cable car [2460] is always running except when under inspection in April and November or during a storm.

Walking times: Kiental – Glütschnessli 2¼ hrs., Glütschnessli – Hohkien 1½ hrs., Hohkien – Schilthorn 3 hrs.; total time 6¾ hrs.

Difference in height: ascent 2000m.

Grade/requirements: fitness test for mountain walkers with bad knees. In places exposed summit ridge with ladders and cables. Marked high mountain path.

Best season: July to October.

Eating places: revolving restaurant on the summit.

Accommodation: in Kiental Hotel Bären

(✆ 033 676 11 21), Chalet (✆ 033 676 16 46). Schilthornhütte; compare Walk 11. Rotstockhütte; compare Walk 13. Hotels in Mürren and Gimmelwald.

Things to look out for: contrast between the idyllic mountain culture of Hohkien and the tourist carousel of Schilthorn. View of the Bernese high Alps, the Black Forest and Vogesen.

Map: 254 T Interlaken, 264 T Jungfrau; 1228 Lauterbrunnen, 1248 Mürren.

Alternatives: descent through the Schilttal to Mürren (3 hrs.), descent through the Engital to the Schilthornhütte (1½ hrs.); continue as in Walk 11. Descent via Rote Härd to the Rotstockhütte on Poganggen (1¾ hrs.); continue as in Walk 13.

Linking walks: 11, 13.

Advice: the fabulous panorama from the Schilthorn can sometimes be shrouded in mist around midday even when there's blue sky. The infernal Triathlon Thun – Schilthorn takes place in the middle of August.

The highest peak of the Bernese foothills lies between the once world famous Lauterbrunnental and the Kiental situated away from the transport and tourism axes. It was on this mountain, which is almost a 3000er, that

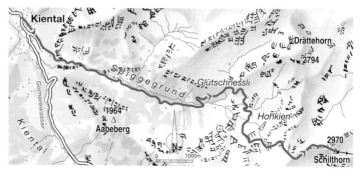

Sunny peak above Mürren – Schlithorn (left) and Bietenhorn (right; Walk 11).

James Bond overwhelmed henchmen and bunnies in the film *'On His Majesty's Secret Service'*. If you fancy being a hero today, climb the Piz Gloria on foot from the rear and only use the cable car for the descent.

From the post bus stop in **Kiental** go up the valley along the hiking path across the valley hillside to the exit of the **Spiggegrund** side valley. Follow a path through the gorge and a roadway to the Spiggebach. Continue south of the stream on the little road along the length of the Spiggegrund. At the end of the valley (Point 1476m) cross another bridge and go along the roadway onto the sunny **Alp Glütschnessli** (1638m). The alpine path winds its way through hollows, over ridges and finally past a waterfall onto **Hohkien** plateau (2026m). Go southwards from the large alpine hut across the plain and steeply uphill onto the karstic high plain of Hart. The path is not always clearly visible but first runs on the level eastwards, then across the southwest side of the Chilchflue up to the **Rote Härd** col (2683m). Cross a slope to the west ridge of the **Schilthorn** and continue along this ridge (cable and ladders) to the concrete, glass and steel construction on **Piz Gloria**.

13 Gspaltenhornhütte, 2455m – Sefinenfurgge, 2612m

The dramatic path over Sefinenfurgge

Griesalp in the Kiental – Gamchi – Gspaltenhornhütte – Sefinenfurgge – Rotstockhütte (Poganggen) – Mürren

Dark clouds over the Gamchi basin – path to the Gspaltenhornhütte.

Starting point: Griesalp (1408m) in the Kiental; post bus [line 300.15] from Reichenbach on the train/bus line Thun-Spiez-Frutigen [301] (only runs June to beginning of October from Kiental village to Griesalp).

Destination: Mürren (1638m); compare Walk 12.

Walking times: Griesalp – Gspaltenhornhütte 3 hrs., hut – Sefinenfurgge 2 hrs., Sefinenfurgge – Poganggen/Rotstockhütte 1 hr., hut – Mürren 2 hrs.; total time 8 hrs.

Difference in height: ascent 1380m, descent 1150m.

Grade/requirements: fitness, sure-footedness and lack of vertigo are necessary; marked, but in places exposed high mountain paths.

Eating places and accommodation: Griesalp: Griesalp mountain hut (✆ 033 676 12 31), Naturfreundehaus Gornere (✆ 033 676 11 40) and the Golderli mountain inn (✆ 033 676 21 92). Gspaltenhornhütte SAC, 75 places, always open, staffed July to Sept., ✆ 033 676 16 29. Rotstockhütte, Stechelberg ski club, 52 places, staffed June to Oct., winter room always open, ✆ 033 855 24 64. Spielbodenalp mountain inn (1793m), ✆ 033 855 14 75.

Things to look out for: the vertical heap of rubble called Gspaltenhorn. An atmospheric evening on Poganggen if the Jungfrau opposite is glowing red .

Map: 264 T Jungfrau; 1248 Mürren.

Alternative: normal path over Sefinenfurgge: shorter, easier, less steep.

Linking walks: 11, 12, 14.

Tip: plan as a two day walk, eg. with an overnight stop in the Rotstockhütte; next day go back into Kiental or through the Schneeige Lücke to Stechelberg. Also walk round Bütlasse – details from Volken/Kundert: *Freie Sicht aufs Gipfelmeer*, Salvioni Edizioni 2003.

The huge valley basin of Gamchi, which has almost been spoilt by a reservoir, Alp Poganggen, on which there is still no service road and the village of Mürren on a sunny terrace and pleasantly free of cars are three areas rescued from industrialisation on the walk over Sefinenfurgge which is more impressive on the 'detour' via the Gspaltenhornhütte than the direct path.

From **Griesalp** go a short way back along the road to the bridge over the Gamchibach. On the alpine road go via the **Golderli** mountain inn and Steinberg to Bürgli and along the hiking path into the **Gamchi** valley basin (1672m). On the left-hand side of the valley (ie. left on ascent) continue up the valley along the marked path to the **Gspaltenhornhütte** (2455m). From the hut along the path return to the junction at Point 2331m (written on a rock: 2½ hrs. to Rotstockhütte). A very exposed path in places crosses ledges out onto the Trogegg, goes along the scree of the Bütlasse northwest face and leads up a steep, slippery path onto the col of a ridge. The path climbs gently over scree slopes and comes out above the **Sefinenfurgge** after crossing a rocky slab (iron rungs) below a cave onto the ridge (about 2660m). Quickly descend onto the pass (2612m). Go along the pass path down to the **Rotstockhütte** (2039m) on Alp Poganggen. Descend the valley on a gentle up-and-down to Bryndli (2025m). The hiking path zigzags steeply down along a ridge and goes left to the **Spielbodenalp** mountain inn. Cross over the Schiltbach and ascend the little road to Gimmela and to **Mürren** (1638m).

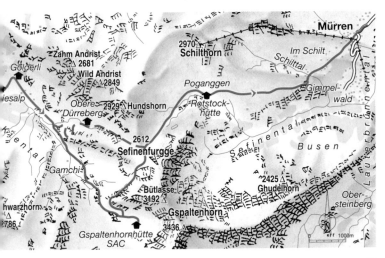

14 Schneeige Lücke, 2360m – Tanzbödeli, 2130m

The Jungfrau as a crag and a character in a novel

Gimmelwald – Sefinental – Chilchbalm – Hindrists Busental – Schneeige Lücke – Busenalp – Tanzbödeli – Busenwald – Stechelberg

Starting point: Gimmelwald (1363m); compare Walk 12.

Destination: Stechelberg (910m); compare Walk 16.

Walking times: Gimmelwald – Chilchbalm 1¾ hrs., Chilchbalm – Schneeige Lücke 2 hrs., Schneeige Lücke – Tanzbödeli 1¼ hrs., Tanzbödeli – Busenalp 30 mins., Busenalp – Stechelberg 1½ hrs.; total time 7 hrs.

Difference in height: ascent 1350m, descent 1700m.

Grade/requirements: demanding mountain walk, in places away from all paths. Sure-footedness and route finding ability are necessary over terrain with no paths. An ice-axe would make the crossing of the Schneeigen Lücke easier.

Best season: July to October.

Eating places: alpine hut on Busenalp (when staffed).

Accommodation: in Gimmelwald Hotel Mittaghorn (✆ 033 855 16 58), Pension Gimmelwald (✆ 033 855 17 30) and Mountain Hostel (✆ 033 855 17 04). In Stechelberg; compare Walk 16.

Things to look out for: Valaisian settlement of Gimmelwald. The highest rock faces in the Bernese Alps after the Eiger North Face. The rugged beauty of the Chilchbalm basin. The dizzying views from Tanzbödeli of the Jungfrau and other peaks.

Map: 264 T Jungfrau; 1248 Mürren.

Alternatives: without Schneeige Lücke, which makes the walk easier and is then classified as red. From Gimmelwald (or Stechelberg) via Busenalp onto Tanzbödeli – or not – and immediately below it across the steep hillside to Obersteinberg; continue as in Walk 15; 5-6 hrs.

Linking walks: 12, 13, 15, 16.

Tip: you can buy Heinrich Clauren's 'Mimili' in an edition by Reclam. And Daniel Anker: Jungfrau – Zauberberg der Männer (Jungfrau – The Magic Mountain of Men), AS-Verlag, Zürich 1996.

'It's a heavenly evening' she whispered softly. The gentle glow of the evening and the heavenly height of the Jungfrau played together in her dark blue eyes and the swan-white breasts rose in her silk bodice! I was overcome with her unimaginable loveliness. I embraced her and, intoxicated by the thrill of the festivities of the evening, I planted a first kiss on her sweet lips. But she sank silently onto my chest and whispered quietly, 'The alps have never inspired me like this before'. The circular walk over Schneeige

Jagged spires in stead of domes – a grassy ridge climbs up onto the flat Tanzbödeli.

Lücke and Tanzbödeli to the Busenalphütte where Wilhelm, the Prussian nobleman, Knight of the iron Cross and lady-killer, kissed the virtuous Oberland country girl, is as breathtaking as this erotic alpine tale from 1819. Walk through the little village from the cable railway station in **Gimmelwald** and along the roadway into the **Sefinental**. Continue as far as the huge valley basin of **Chilchbalm** (about 1580m) where the path stops. Cross over the various tributaries of the Sefinen Lütschine at suitable places, which is not always easy due to the possible remains of avalanche snow at the foot of the north faces of Gspaltenhorn and Tschingelspitz. At about 1680m the ascent begins across a steep grassy hillside into the **Hindrists Busental** (keeping first left then right; some tracks and waymarkers). You now reach a flat area strewn with large boulders. Continue across scree, keeping as far as possible on the left of the valley (danger of ice and rock fall from the Tschingelgrat), up into the **Schneeige Lücke** (about 2360m) south of the Ghudelhorn. Descend over scree into the Vordrists Busental, to about 2140m, then eastwards up into a notch (about 2190m) south of the Schafhorn. Carry on along tracks, keeping diagonally right below the steep flanks of Ellstab and Spitzhorn down to the path which comes up from the Busenalphütte (at Point 1933m). Go eastwards along this to the Busenegg (no name on the map) where you reach an official hiking path again. Continue a short way up along this until the path turns off right to the **Tanzbödeli**. It leads round a rib and across a steep grassy hillside onto this viewing terrace (about 2130m) below the Spitzhorn. Return to Point 1933m on the Alp Busen and down to the **Busenalphütte** (1841m; Gsodboden on the map). Going eastwards on the path again return to the hiking path which descends precipitously through the Busenwald into the **Sefinental**. Go down the valley at first on the level, then steeply down to **Stechelberg**.

Also conquered by authors – the Jungfrau in the evening sun.

15 Hinteres Lauterbrunnental

Delicate flowers, icy north faces, wild streams, romantic mountain hotels

Stechelberg – Trachsellauenen – Schmadribach – Oberhornsee – Obersteinberg – Folla – Stechelberg

Starting point and destination: Stechelberg (910m); compare Walk 16.
Walking times: Stechelberg – Schmadribach 4 hrs., Schmadribach – Oberhornsee 45 mins., Oberhornsee – Obersteinberg 45 mins., descent to Stechelberg 2 hrs.; total time 7½ hrs.
Difference in height: 1300m.
Grade/requirements: long, waymarked,

not very difficult mountain walk with several places to stop and eat and stay overnight. In bad visibility the route finding is quite difficult near the Oberhorn moraine.
Best season: end of June to October.
Accommodation: in Stechelberg: compare Walk 16. Mountain hotels: Trachsellauenen (✆ 033 855 12 35), Obersteinberg (& 033 855 20 33), Tschingelhorn on Folla (✆ 033 855 13 43); all open May/June to September/October. Schmadrihütte (2262m), self catering hut of the Akademischer Alpenclub Bern, 14 places, always open.
Things to look out for: nature and culture in rare harmony.
Map: 264 T Jungfrau; 1248 Mürren.
Alternatives: direct ascent from Trachsellauenen via Schürboden, Läger, Im Tal and Schafläger to Oberhornsee; 3½ hrs. (this is the route of the Timberland Way completed in 1994). Descent from Obersteinberg via Tanzbödeli and Busenalp into the Sefinental; compare Walk 14.
Linking walks: 13, 14, 16.
Tip: due to the afternoon sun, walk in the given direction. A good brochure to the Hinteres Lauterbrunnental is available from the tourist office in Lauterbrunnen.

Mountain farmers (the Schürboden hut dating from 1805 is a jewel), mountain climbers (Welzenbach routes on the north faces of the Gletscherhorn, Grosshorn and Breithorn), miners (Trachsellauenen furnaces and miner's house renovated in 1993/94; tunnels accessible at your own risk), mountain hotels (the Obersteinberg hotel is one of the most charming in the Oberland), mountain streams (the Schmadribachfall was once almost as famous as the Staubbachfall) are the special features of this walk.
From **Stechelberg** go along the mule path up the valley, at first on the left of the Weisse Lütschine, then from Sichellauenen on the right via **Trachsellauenen** (1202m) to Schürboden (Scheuerboden, 1377m). Follow the yellow and green

marked Timberland Way of the Swiss organisation for nature conservation, keeping left across two torrents, up to the turn-off for the Holdri waterfall (it's worth a detour). Just afterwards turn off left again and go steeply uphill along a newly made dirt path in places round many bends to reach the hut path up to the Schmadrihütte which comes over from the Schwand huts (danger of ice-fall). Go diagonally across the steep stepped hillside onto a scree-covered flat area near the **Schmadribach** where the path to the Schmadrihütte (2262m) turns off (150 vertical metres, 30 mins.). Go westwards on the stony path onto the Oberhorn moraine (about 2150m), almost down to the Alp Oberhorn (2029m) and along the Chrummbach to the **Oberhornsee** (2065m). Descend to Schafläger, across the Tschingel Lütschine and the precipitous hillside to the **Obersteinberg** mountain hotel (1778m). Cross the hillside along the high mountain path via the **Hotel Tschingelhorn** onto **Folla** (1678m) until you reach the end of the Sefinental. Steep descent to **Stechelberg**.

Simply overwhelming – nature reserve of the Hinteres Lauterbrunnental.

16 Rottalhütte, 2755m

To the Unesco World Natural Heritage Jungfrau – Aletsch – Bietschhorn

Stechelberg – Altläger – Bäreflue – Rottalhütte – Stechelberg

Starting point and destination: Stechelberg (910m); post bus [line 311.15] from Lauterbrunnen; there by train [311] from Interlaken East.

Walking times: ascent 5½ hrs., descent 4 hrs.; total time 9½ hrs.

Difference in height: ascent and descent both 1850m.

Grade: hard mountain walk over precipitous terrain. Key point is a steep gully with a danger of rockfall (cable); also three other places require the utmost care. Marked path except on the descent

from Altläger.

Best season: July to Sept.; quietest in autumn when new snow prevents alpinists from making trips into the high mountains.

Accommodation: Rottalhütte SAC, 45 places, always open, staffed at weekends in the high season, ✆ 033 855 24 45. In Stechelberg: Hotel Stechelberg (✆ 033 855 29 21), Naturfreundehaus Alpenhof (✆ 033 855 12 02).

Things to look out for: the view of the Hinteres Lauterbrunnental. The creaking of the glacier. The Jungfrau close by.

Map: 264 T Jungfrau; 1248 Mürren, 1249 Finsteraarhorn.

Linking walks: 14, 15, 17.

Important advice: don't make a stop between Altläger and Bäreflue where ice could avalanche down from the Jungfrau, nor at the rock where it says '½ way to the Rottalhütte'. Stop instead at the ruins of an alpine building (Point 1937m).

'As far as the eye can see and one's bold step might penetrate, everything lies buckled and twisted in dreadful devastation.' This discovery of the place where today's Rottalhütte is located, did not stop Franz Josef Hugi, the grammar school teacher and geologist from Solothurn, from pushing on with his guides into the wild and dramatic Rottal four times from 1827 to 1830 or from building a very simple shelter and attempting an ascent of the Jungfrau – one reason why the Rottal is a legendary place in the Bernese Oberland. Today it is a sheer, vertical ascent on narrow paths from the apple trees up to the vegetation line, right into the middle of the first Unesco World Natural Heritage in the Alps.

From **Stechelberg** go along the mule path east of the Lütschine 400m up the valley to the left turn-off for the marked hut path at the Staldenbach. It leads steeply up to the rocks of the Staldenflue and runs along this on a sometimes exposed ledge to the **Alp Altläger** (1580m); this path was used by the farmers when they used to move up onto the high meadows for the summer. The path continues to zigzag up to the Schafbach, crosses over it

What a location! View of Tschingelhorn, Doldenhorn and Blüemlisalp (from the left).

and follows a moraine via Point 1937 past the Silberhornhütte turn-off to the **Bäreflue** which, since 1977, can be overcome at a new place protected from icefall. The route goes through a steep gully of friable rock which you only see at the last minute and where there are cables to help you climb through. Go along the grassy 'roof' of the Bäreflue to a shoulder above the Rottal glacier. Continue eastwards on and above the moraine over partly precipitous ground to the **Rottalhütte** which you finally reach up some rock steps. The descent to **Altläger** goes along the same route. From the hut follow an unmarked, overgrown path southwards down towards the Schafbach where the path joins from Alp Stuefestein. Carry on north-westwards at first for a short way across alpine meadows, then across rock strewn slopes (cables) down to Sichellouwena; this path is the so-called 'footpath', the fast connecting route for alpine dairymen from the valley onto the alpine pasture. Eventually return along the mule path to **Stechelberg**.

17 Staubbachfall and Trümmelbachfälle

Powerful and dramatic wonder of nature in the 'Yosemite Valley' of the Alps

Lauterbrunnen – Staubbachfall – Trümmelbachfälle – Stechelberg

Starting point: Lauterbrunnen (795m); compare Walk 11.

Destination: Stechelberg (910m); Walk 16.

Walking times: Lauterbrunnen – Staubbachfall 30 mins., onward path to the Trümmelbachfälle 30 mins., Trümmelbachfälle ½-1½ hrs., path to Stechelberg 1¼ hrs.; total time around 3 hrs.

Difference in height: a good 100m.

Grade/requirements: none.

Best season: May to July; Trümmelbachfälle open daily 8.00/9.00 to 5.00/6.00 from April to Nov. The walk is always possible.

Eating places and accommodation: hotels in Lauterbrunnen. Hotel Trümmelbach (ⓒ 033 855 32 32). In Stechelberg; compare Walk 16.

Things to look out for: the Staubbachfall is, with a 287m drop, the highest waterfall in Switzerland. The Trümmelbachfälle, Europe's only glacial waterfalls in the heart of the mountains. The Mürrenbach falls, whose cascades plunge over 600m in total.

Map: 254 T Interlaken, 264 T Jungfrau; 1228 Lauterbrunnen, 1248 Mürren.

Alternatives: just go as far as the Trümmelbachfälle. Or from there ascend to Wengen (see Walk 20).

Linking walks: 12, 14, 15, 16, 17, 20.

Tip: do not forget your jumper and anorak. The Staubbach waterfall is at its most beautiful in the morning sun.

'The pure jet / leaps from the lofty / precipitous rock face,/ then rises in cloud-waves / of sweet spray / against the smooth rock, / and gently caught, / it flows veil-like, / softly murmurous, / down to the depths below.'

If Johann Wolfgang von Goethe had seen not only the Staubbachfall, but also the thundering Trümmelbachfälle in the heart of the mountains as they transport 20,000 tons of debris from the Eiger, Mönch and Jungfrau each year, then his poem 'Song of the Spirits over the waters' would have sounded more dramatic. But these falls only became accessible in 1877 and the lowest of them (there are ten altogether) not until 1990.

From **Lauterbrunnen** station go along the road into the village. At the point where it turns down to the left, carry straight on along a little road to the cemetery. Carry on along the path, which was reopened in summer 1997, onto the Staubbachhubel and into the 100m long gallery behind the waterfall. Return to the little tarmac road and go up the valley to Bir Buechen. On the hiking path right cross the valley bottom and go over the Weisse Lütschine and the Trümmelbach to the post bus stop, restaurant and entrance. Take the lift up inside the mountain, and visit the upper **Trümmelbachfälle** first, then the lower ones. Afterwards go 500m along the main road in the direction of Stechelberg as far as a campsite. Go through this and change over onto the other side of the valley. On the west of the Weisse Lütschine go along a little road, then take a footpath past the Mürrenbach and other waterfalls to **Stechelberg**.

The thundering of the spirits in the water – up to 20,000 litres per second.

18 Eiger glacier, 2320m

Lots of sights along an old and yet new path

Wengen – Biglenalp – Eigergletscher – Kleine Scheidegg

Starting point: Wengen (1275m); train [line 311] from Interlaken East via Lauterbrunnen.
Destination: Kleine Scheidegg (2061m); train to Lauterbrunnen [311] or Grindelwald [312].
Walking times: Wengen – Stalden 1½ hrs., Stalden – Biglenalp 45 mins., Biglenalp – Eiger glacier 2 hrs., descent onto Kleine Scheidegg 30 mins.; total time 4¾ hrs.
Difference in height: ascent 1050m, descent 260m.
Grade/requirements: mountain walk on marked paths throughout.
Best season: June to Oct/Nov.
Eating places: on the Eiger glacier.
Accommodation: hotels in Wengen. Eiger glacier; compare Walk 19. Kleine

Scheidegg; compare Walk 20.
Things to look out for: the twelve Staubbach benches; the old Mittellegihütte; the ice-covered faces and avalanches of the Jungfrau and Mönch; the North Face of the Eiger from Kleine Scheidegg.
Map: 254 T Interlaken, 264 T Jungfrau; 1228 Lauterbrunnen, 1229 Grindelwald, 1249 Finsteraarhorn.
Alternatives: leave the Eiger glacier on the right and climb directly up onto Kleine Scheidegg (saving 1 hr.). Descent by the normal route to Wengen (1¾ hrs.).
Advice: the Jungfrau-Marathon from Interlaken via Lauterbrunnen, Wengen and Eiger glacier onto Kleine Scheidegg takes place at the beginning of September.
Linking walks: 19, 20.

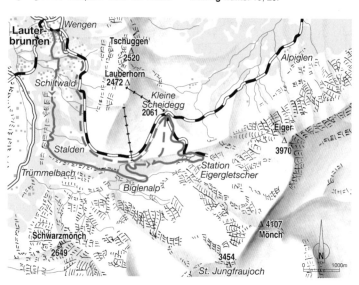

A place to while away some time – Staubach benches at Wengen.

'Up on the meadows, where you only meet shepherds in the middle of summer regaling the travellers with milk products, the majestic summit of the Eiger is right in front of you.' Here today, you meet people with shepherd-like clothing all year round. They welcome tourists from all over the world who have come here to take a cog railway through the Eiger onto the Jungfraujoch. The meadows right at the top are called Kleine Scheidegg and their first famous tourist crossing was made in 1771 by the Englishmen Norton Nichols, the philosopher Karl Viktor von Bonstetten and Jakob Samuel Wyttenbach, scientist and priest at the church of the Holy Spirit in Bern. The latter published the first travel guide to the Bernese Oberland in 1777 (unfortunately not translated into English). Its title *'Short introduction for those making a journey through part of the most curious alpine regions of the Lauterbrunnenthal, Grindelwald, and return via Meyringen to Bern'*.

Go a few paces above **Wengen** station under the track, down through the village and along the little road up the valley on the level to **Schiltwald** and to the **Staubbachbänkli**. Ascend a short way uphill, then follow a very beautiful (forest) path up the valley, at first flat, but later climbing up to the crossroads on **Stalden** (1666m). Keep along a roadway to the Alp Mettla and along the high mountain path onto the western **Biglenalp** (1707m). Go a short way along the Trümmelbach and take the path left that runs up onto the ridge which comes down from the Eiger glacier. This brings you to the **Eiger glacier station**. Walk along beside the track of the Jungfrau train down onto **Kleine Scheidegg**.

Grindelwald valley: glacier and inns

'Like a gigantic slice of plum cake' is how Daniel P. Rhodes describes the Kleine Fiescherhorn in *'A Pleasure-Book of Grindelwald'*. And the Wetterhorn was for him 'a celestial Chartres; and those broad shafts of crimson light dashing against its sides might almost be heard, like the trumpet blasts of an angelic procession.' The whole *'Pleasure-Book of Grindelwald'* that appeared in 1903 is not as poetic. But everyone is filled with awe as they look at the high massif from Grindelwald and has been for more than 250 years.

'Everyone who travels through Switzerland wants to see Grindelwald and then says, he has been to the Alps,' wrote Carl Gottlob Küttner in 1785 in his 'letters of a Saxon from Switzerland'. A visit to its glaciers is a must when visiting Grindelwald, especially the glacier gorge at the Lower Grindelwald Glacier (Walk 21). Its coolness is especially pleasant if the freezing level has been lying for a week on the top of the Finsteraarhorn (4273m). Global warming is again responsible for the Upper Grindelwald glacier retreating every year by 50 to 60m; it is still one of the deepest penetrating alpine glaciers, but the grotto can't be excavated any more to show tourists the inside of the seemingly constant ice. From the mountain station of the Pfingstegg cable railway it ambles along gently to the Stieregg (1650m) above the Lower Grindelwald glacier. This is where, in 1823, the first alpine accommodation was built in the Bernese Oberland, the Stieregghütte – from here there are wonderful views of the high alpine scenery: Fiescherwand is very close by, but even closer is the ice cream on the plate.

Other famous places for mountain accommodation in the Alps are the Berghotel on the 2680m high Faulhorn (Walks 24 to 26) where royal families have marvelled at the sunrise, or Hotel Gleckstein (Walk 22) which was originally built as an intermediate stop for the planned cable car from Hotel Wetterhorn onto the Wetterhorn summit. Thankfully only the lower section of this cable car was built (and then torn down again). Anyway, there are enough trains putting within reach the mountains around Grindelwald – amongst others, a cog railway rattles through the Eiger and Mönch onto the Jungfraujoch (3454m), the highest station in Europe. In short, Grindelwald is one of the meccas of tourist and alpine development in the Alps.

The sheer contrast between the famously notorious faces of the Alps (the North Face of the Eiger with its 28 routes) and the well-trodden high mountain paths from the Männlichen onto Kleine Scheidegg (Walk 19) or from Schynigen Platte to the Faulhorn, is always a refreshing and pleasurable sight. The Eiger and the other peaks shoot up into the sky in such an awesome way that the ugliness caused by new buildings in particular and the tourist trade in general are no longer so conspicuous.

Gottlieb Strasser, better known as a priest of the glacier, made this criticism

Fiescherwand and Unterer Grindelwald glacier have impressed tourists since time immemorial.

during his creative period from 1879 to 1912: 'You can hardly see the mountains for palaces!' Without its 3000er and 4000er, Grindelwald, situated at 1000m, would certainly not be one of the most popular summer and winter resorts in the Alps or perhaps even in the world – the many tourists who journey at all times of the year and in all weathers onto the Jungfraujoch underline this fact. The announcements when, for example, the train reaches 'Eismeer' station, are given not only in German, French and Italian but also in English, Spanish, Japanese, Chines and Korean.

19 Männlichen, 2342m – Eiger Trail

Opposite and below the world famous North Face

(Wengen or Grindelwald) – Männlichen mountain station – Männlichen – Kleine Scheidegg – Station Eiger glacier – Alpiglen

Location: Wengen (1275m); see Walk 18; Grindelwald (1034m); see Walk 20.
Starting point: Männlichen mountain station (2229m); cable car from Wengen (end of May to end of Oct.) or cable car (beginning of June to mid-Oct.) from Grindelwald-Grund (943m); 20 mins. from the centre.
Destination: Alpiglen (1616m); with the Jungfraubahn [312] down to Grindelwald.
Walking times: 4½ hrs., including 2 hrs. for the Eiger Trail.
Difference in height: ascent 440m, descent 1050m.
Grade/requirements: the path Männlichen – Kleine Scheidegg – Eiger glacier is extremely easy, you need to be sure-footed for the Eiger Trail.
Best season: June to Oct. Do not start the Eiger Trail until the afternoon.
Eating places and accommodation: Männlichen Berghaus (℡ 033 853 10 68).

Kleine Scheidegg; see Walk 20. Guesthouse Eigergletscher (℡ 079 456 36 39). Hotel des Alpes, Alpiglen (℡ 033 853 11 30).
Things to look out for: Hinterstoisser Traverse, Death Bivouac, Traverse of the Gods, The Spider. See Daniel Anker: Eiger – The Vertical Arena, The Mountaineers 2000.
Map: 254 T Interlaken; 1229 Grindelwald.
Alternatives: from Wengen on foot along the breathtaking path onto the Männlichen (3¼ hrs.). From Grindelwald on foot in 4¾ hrs. From Wart there's a moderate Klettersteig (via ferrata) right at the edge of the North Face onto the Rotstock (2663m); 1½ hrs. Descent back to Eiger glacier station. You can hire the specific equipment for Klettersteig in Grindelwald.
Linking walks: 18, 20.
Tip: by mountainbike from Grindelwald; tarmac road to Männlichen mountain hut.

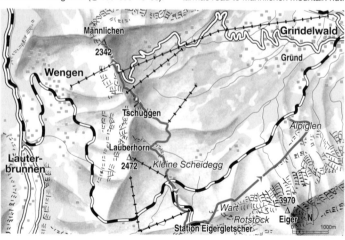

Box seat for the spider – view from the Eiger Trail up to the wall of walls.

What the Matterhorn is to Zermatt, the North Face of the Eiger is to Grindelwald – the mountains as a chamber of horrors. The Eiger would not have become so famous if accidents on the North Face had not always provided the headlines. Tourists jostle around the telescopes at the Berghaus Männlichen and on Kleine Scheidegg and they cause traffic jams on the hiking motorway Männlichen – Kleine Scheidegg, as well as on the Eiger Trail, opened in 1997 at the foot of the North Face. Looking out from the security of the terrace at the insecurity of nature tourism has functioned according to this pattern since its beginnings. Wilderness and civilisation. Have some adventures, but please, at some distance and with a return ticket in your pocket. From the **mountain railway station** at **Männlichen** take the hiking path on the south ridge in 15 mins. to the summit of **Männlichen** – a very worthwhile detour. Return and go along the broad high mountain path below Tschuggen onto **Kleine Scheidegg** (2061m). More or less along the tracks of the Jungfraubahn continue up to the **Eiger glacier station** (2320m) where the train disappears into the stomach of the Eiger. The Eiger Trail begins at the station and goes onto the north side of Rotstock where you can touch Eiger rock. A little later the path climbs up onto the grassy knoll of **Wart**. Going right across the grassy and scree-covered foothills of the Eiger face, it then descends steadily. Finally, when you are at the forest boundary, you come to a signpost: you could continue right, descending to the Grindelwald glacier gorge, left goes to **Alpiglen**.

20 Kleine Scheidegg, 2061m

Under the magic of the Eiger, Mönch and Jungfrau

Grindelwald – Alpiglen – Kleine Scheidegg – Wengernalp – Wengen and Lauterbrunnen or Trümmelbach

Starting point: Grindelwald (1034m); train [line 312] from Interlaken East.
Destination: Lauterbrunnen (795m) or Trümmelbach (819m); compare Walk 15.
Walking times: Grindelwald – Alpiglen 2¼ hrs., Alpiglen – Kleine Scheidegg 1½ hrs., Scheidegg – Wengernalp 30 mins., Wengernalp – Wengen 1¾ hrs., Wengen – Lauterbrunnen 1¼ hrs., Wengernalp – Trümmelbach 2½ hrs.; total time 7¼ hrs.
Difference in height: ascent 1100m, descent 1350m.
Grade: easy, long, waymarked, but the adventurous descent to Trümmelbach is only suitable for surefooted mountain walkers with a lack of vertigo (graded red!)
Best season: June to November (without

the often icy descent to Trümmelbach).
Eating places and accommodation: hotels in Grindelwald, Wengen, Lauterbrunnen and Trümmelbach. Hotel des Alpes, Alpiglen (✆ 033 853 11 30). Kleine Scheidegg: Scheidegg Hotels (✆ 033 855 12 12), Röstizzeria-Bahnhof (✆ 033 855 11 51), Grindelwaldblick (✆ 033 855 13 74). Hotel Jungfrau, Wengernalp (✆ 033 855 16 22).
Things to look out for: north faces, mountain railways, Lütschinen valleys, waterfalls.
Map: 254 T Interlaken, 264 T Jungfrau; 1228 Lauterbrunnen, 1229 Grindelwald, 1248 Mürren.
Linking walks: 11, 17, 18, 19, 21, 27, 30.
Tip: Daniel Anker: Mönch – Mittelpunkt im Dreigestirn, AS Verlag, Zürich 2002.

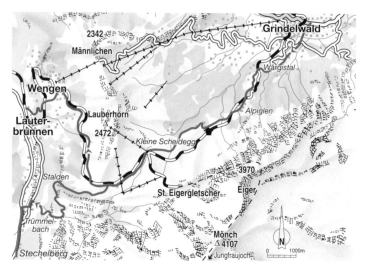

Classic destination below the Eiger and Mönch: train intersection on Kleine Scheidegg.

The history of alpinism and tourism was written on the Eiger (3970m), Mönch (4107m) and Jungfrau (4158m) with the first ascent of the Jungfrau in 1811, north bastion of the Mönch in 1866, North Face of the Eiger in 1938 and the opening of the Jungfraujoch train in 1912.

From **Grindelwald** station go a short way into the village, down along the road in the direction of Grund, but at Gasthof Glacier keep left and descend the road to the bridge over the Schwarze Lütschine (951m). Now following the signposts for Alpiglen go through the Grindelwald district of Wärgistal on roads, roadways and footpaths. From **Alpiglen** (1616m) at first continue beside the Wengernalp railway, then go over to the Arvengarten and up onto **Kleine Scheidegg**. Carry on along beside the railway line onto **Wengernalp** (1874m). The paths split here: either continue along the tracks to Wengen (1275m) and down the zigzag path to **Lauterbrunnen**, or go along the footpath, crossing the roadway, down to **Alp Mettla** and along the roadway on the level to the crossroads at **Stalden** (1665m). Go to the left and southwards to the upper and lower Preech mountain pasture. The narrow path descends to the bottom of the deeply-cut valley of the Trümmelbach and crosses this on a footbridge. Ascend for a short way on the other side. The path zigzags steeply down into the Lauterbrunnen valley and at the lowest point goes across a rock ledge out of which the path has been cut (cable). Continue through a meadow to the valley road and then to the right to **Trümmelbach** – or to the left in about an hour to **Stechelberg**.

21 Upper and Lower Grindelwald glacier

Cool walk for hot days

Hotel Wetterhorn – Gletscherbar – Milchbach – Gesteinslehrpfad – Pfingstegg – Stieregg – Grindelwald

Location and destination: Grindelwald (1034m); compare Walk 20.
Starting point: Hotel Wetterhorn (1230m); compare Walk 22.
Walking times: Hotel Wetterhorn – Gletscherbar 45 mins., Gletscherbar – Milchbach 45 mins., Milchbach – Pfingstegg 30 mins., Pfingstegg – Stieregg 1 hr., Stieregg – Grindelwald 2 hrs. total time 5 hrs.
Difference in height: ascent around 750m, descent around 950m.
Grade/requirements: for fairly vertigo-free hikers; if you don't trust your old knees on the descent into the valley, take the Pfingstegg cable car (runs from June to Oct.). Well-marked path throughout.
Best season: June to October; the staircase to the Gletscherbar is open from May onwards.
Eating places: Gletscherbar, Milchbach,

Pfingstegg restaurants, glacier gorge.
Accommodation: Hotel Wetterhorn ✆ 033 853 12 18. Restaurant Stieregg, 16 places, open June to October, ✆ 033 853 17 66. Berghaus Marmorbruch, ✆ 033 853 13 18.
Alternatives: 1) from Restaurant Milchbach along the Leiternweg (path constructed with ladders) for which you have to pay a toll, up to the Undren Wächsel (about 1600m) in the middle of a unique world of rock and ice, grass and water (there and back 1½ hrs.). 2) from Stieregg along an alpine path protected in places to the Schreckhornhütte (2528m); 3½ hrs. 3) from the fork at Point 1381m via Berghaus Marmorbruch to the restaurant in the Gletscherschlucht; after seeing these sights go either on foot or by bus into the village of Grindelwald.
Things to look out for: wooden steps on the polished rock (entrance fee). Informative rock path where you will be amazed at the rock strata lying on top of each other, some of which date back to about 100 million years ago (free).
Map: 254 T Interlaken; 1229 Grindelwald.
Linking walks: 20, 22, 30.
Tip: summer toboggan run on Pfingstegg.

To stay in Grindelwald without a trip to at least one of the natural sights which gave the furthermost settlement in the valley of the Schwarze Lütschine the nickname of Gletscherdorf (glacier village), would be like staying in London without a visit to the Tower Bridge. From **Hotel Wetterhorn** take the broad forest path (the turn-off to the ruins of the valley station of the

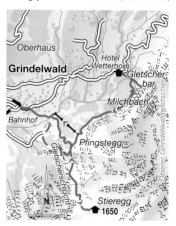

Behind the Gletscherbar, but where is the ice?

Wetterhorn lift is on the way; compare Walk 22) over to the foot of the apex where the **Gletscherbar** (1373m) is enthroned. A wooden staircase makes its way up over the rock striations (890 steps; 150 vertical metres). At the top you can see the ever-retreating tongue of the Upper Grindelwald glacier. In the summer of 2000 there was still an ice grotto you could visit here. Go back down the steps, along another broad path to the bridge (1212m) across the Schwarze Lütschine and on a winding path up to the **Restaurant Milchbach** (1348m) on Halsegg. An informative rock path leads you high across the north west flank of the Mättenberg to the mountain station of **Pfingstegg cable car** (1391m). There are some explanatory notes on a board at the Breitlouwina slabs.

From Pfingstegg go along the high mountain path into the valley of the Lower Grindelwald glacier to **Restaurant Stieregg** (1650m). Back at the fork at Point 1381m, descend fairly steeply, then more on the level to Halten and to the Mättenberg bridge (986m). Continue along a road, then take a footpath up to the **Grindelwald** village road.

22 Glecksteinhütte, 2317m

Dizzying journey into the heart of the high mountains

Gleckstein bus stop – Engi – Glecksteinhütte – Hotel Wetterhorn

Location: Grindelwald (1034m); → Walk 20.
Starting point: Gleckstein bus stop (1540m) on the bus route [312.20] Grindelwald-Hotel Wetterhorn-Grosse Scheidegg.
Destination: Hotel Wetterhorn (1230m), Oberer Gletscher bus stop.
Walking times: ascent 2¾ hrs., descent 2¼ hrs.; total time 5 hrs.
Difference in height: ascent 910m, descent 1220m.
Grade: good, exposed, and at times protected mountain path; tricky when wet. Only for sure-footed, vertigo-free hikers.

Best season: June to October.
Eating places and accommodation: Hotel Wetterhorn; compare Walk 21. Glecksteinhütte SAC, 100 places, always open, staffed July to Sept., ✆ 033 853 11 40.
Things to look out for: ibex, glaciers, path construction (on Zybach slabs puzzling steps left and right of the path).
Map: 254 T Interlaken; 1229 Grindelwald.
Alternatives: ascent from Hotel Wetterhorn 1 hr. longer. The section between Grindelwald – Hotel Wetterhorn on foot (one hour each way).
Linking walks: 21, 30.
Advice: if there's a danger of the glacier rupturing, then the approach from Gleckstein bus stop is closed.
Tip: a lift cage near Hotel Wetterhorn; the ruins of the valley station near the path to the Oberer Gletscher. You can read more on that in the beautifully illustrated books by R. Rubi: Im Tal von Grindelwald – Vom Bergbauerndorf zum Fremdenort, Der Sommer- und Winterkurort, Das Gletscherdorf; all published by Verlag Sutter, Grindelwald (only available in German).

The local Grindelwald newspaper reported on 17. Feb. 1944 that a licence had been granted for a mountain lift to be built from Hotel Wetterhorn near Grindelwald to the Glecksteinhütte on the Wetterhorn, half of the proposed lift to the top of the Haslijungfrau. On 27. July 1908 the first cable car in the world to carry people was put into operation. The second section to the Hotel Gleckstein, dating from 1904, was never built and the Wetterhorn lift came to a standstill in 1915. There's a replica of the lift cage near Hotel Wetterhorn, a memorial to the technical conquest of the high mountains. But in the 1990s there were storm clouds brewing on the Wetterhorn when Grindelwald was planning the construction of a cable car to run past the Wetterhorn onto the Rosenhorn (3689m) in order to develop a snow-safe skiing area in the middle of a protected landscape.

From **Gleckstein bus stop** climb a little way up to the vertical precipices of the Wetterhorn bastion. The protected Isch path extends to **Engi** (1735m).

Supposed to have been conquered by cable car – the Wetterhorn, the symbol of Grindelwald.

Above the remains of the former mountain station (1670m) of the Wetterhorn lift – it's worth making a detour there – go into the valley of the Upper Grindelwald glacier. At first descend, then ascend across the steep hillside up the valley. The Wyssbach waterfall acts as a shower and the traverse of the Zybach slabs proves to be a dizzy-making experience. The exposed path above overcomes a last obstacle before crossing sheep pastures to reach the **Glecksteinhütte**, the Hotel Gleckstein dating from 1904 which has been repeatedly extended. The descent is the same as the ascent, but after leaving the northwest flank of the Wetterhorn, descend left to **Hotel Wetterhorn**.

71

23 Schynige Platte – Geiss, 2067m

The most dramatic and exciting ascent with an abundance of flowers and views of the Schynige Platte and its southernmost peak Geiss

Gsteigwiler – Bürgle – Bigelti – Schynige Platte – Geiss

Starting point: Gsteigwiler (647m) at the exit of the Lütschinen valleys. Bus [line 300.80] from Interlaken West via Wilderswil.
Destination: Schynige Platte (1967m); compare Walk 24.
Walking times: Gsteigwiler – Schynige Platte – Geiss 4½ hrs.

Difference in height: ascent 1420m, descent 100m.
Grade/requirements: for relatively fit, sure-footed hikers with route finding experience. The path is marked sparingly and is overgrown in places outside the forest. The route is not suitable for a descent.
Best season: at the most beautiful end of June/beginning of July when many of the alpine flowers are in bloom.
Eating places and accommodation: Hotel Schynige Platte (© 033 822 34 31).
Things to look out for: ascent across mostly vegetated steps. Informative alpine garden. Wonderful panorama.
Map: 254 T Interlaken; 1228 Lauterbrunnen.
Alternative: from Zweilütschinen station along the hiking path on the right of the Lütschine to the turn-off by the Rufibach; 15 mins. longer than from Gsteigwiler.
Tip: sunrise trips in summer.
Linking walks: 9, 24.

Since 1893 a rack railway has run from Wilderswil onto Schynige Platte, the much praised viewpoint high above the confluence of the Lütschinen valleys. For the 1,400 vertical and the 7,257 track metres the train today takes 50 minutes. Between the mountain station and Geiss, not named on the map, one of the three peaks of Schynige Platte, lies an alpine garden; there are 500 different flowering plants and ferns over an area of 8323 sq. m. If you would like to see the alpine flowers in their wild environment, you should choose the little used path from Gsteigweiler across the steep southwest side onto Schynige Platte.

From the terminus in **Gsteigwiler** go up the valley along a road to the other side of the Rufigrabe where, at a barbecue site, a broad path branches off. Gently ascend this path and 250m after the bend in the wood the mountain agricultural path turns off right. Going over a rock step, it leads to the Under and Ober **Bürgle** (1104m). The path continues past the hut and zigzags across scrawny meadows and through a forest to the uppermost hut of **Scharte** (about 1400m). Now go eastwards to a rock step where the narrow path becomes exposed. Cross over onto the south side of a steep U-shaped valley and ascend through this to the alpine meadows of **Bigelti**. Do not go right over to the alpine buildings, instead climb directly up to the official hiking path. Continue along this to Hotel **Schynige Platte** (about 1980m). Before quenching your thirst at the hotel, go quickly up onto the **Geiss**.

Schynige Platte's paradise of flowers – Maragon lily at the edge of an isolated path.

24 Schynige Platte – Faulhorn, 2680m – First

Not only the path, but also three summits are your objective

Schynige Platte – Tuba – Oberberghorn – Egg – Männdlenen – Faulhorn – Bachsee – First

Location: Wilderswil (584m); train [line 311/ 312] from Interlaken Ost.
Starting point: Schynige Platte (1967m); rack railway [314] from Wilderswil; in service from June to October.
Destination: First (2166m); by cable car (end of May to the end of October) to Grindelwald (1034m); train from there [312] to Interlaken Ost.
Walking times: Schynige Platte – Oberberghorn 1 hr., Oberberghorn – Egg 1 hr., Egg – Männdlenen 45 mins., Männdlenen – Faulhorn 1¼ hrs., Faulhorn – First 1½ hrs.; total time 5½ hrs.
Difference in height: ascent about 800m, descent about 600m.
Grade: the direct high mountain path to the Faulhorn is easy but stony. The very worthwhile way via Tuba and Oberberghorn is narrow in places and rather ex-

posed. Sure-footedness is essential.
Best season: June to October.
Eating places: First mountain restaurant.
Accommodation: Schynige Platte; see Walk 23. Berghütte Männdlenen/ Weberhütte, from the end of June to the middle of Oct., (✆ 033 853 44 64). Faulhorn; see Walk 26.
Things to look out for: the view down to Interlaken, the Bernese High Alps.
Map: 254 T Interlaken; 1228 Lauterbrunnen, 1229 Grindelwald.
Alternative: take the direct route to Loucherhorn missing out Tuba and Oberberghorn.
Linking walks: 23, 25, 26, 27, 28, 29.
Tip: moonshine walk, one to three times a year. Information on Jungfrau regional trains, Reisedienst (Travel Service), ✆ 033 828 72 33; information about planning a walk, ✆ 033 828 73 51.

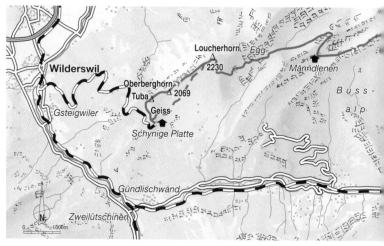

Detour from the panoramic path – wooden ladder onto the Oberberghorn.

A first class trip for everyone – whole armies of people hike the six hours from the Alpengarten to the oldest Grindelwald mountain hotel and along the Bachsee to First. Even more unforgettable is the experience if you do this popular walk in the moonshine. One to three times each summer the rack railway climbs up late at night onto Schynige Platte full of hikers who only have one aim in mind – to watch sunset on the Faulhorn (see Walk 26). If, on the other hand, you are walking during the day, you should definitely take the panoramic path from Schynige Platte to the two viewing summits of Tuba and Obergberghorn.

Embodiment of the Oberland – Bachsee with its high mountain backdrop.

From **Schynige Platte** terminus walk to the Hotel and along the panoramic path, west below the tower of the Gumihorn, onto **Tuba** (2076m). Continue along the airy ridge down onto a col. Shortly afterwards a path branches off left. Ascend **Oberberghorn** (2069m), up some ladders at the top. Back on the path, continue round the Oberberghorn. The path continues to follow the ridge between the alpine pastures on the right and the sheer drop on the left. Just

Tired legs down on the Brienzersee – view back from the Giessbach boat quay.

dress circle of this natural theatre.' After all this bathos we leave the Faulhorn and descend northwards to the Brienzersee.

From the **Faulhorn** descend westwards onto a flat area. Go across Fulegg down onto the **Bonerenweng** col (2282m) and continue downhill to the right, over the alpine meadows of Hübschenmatten and across the limestone gullies of the Bättenalp to **Gstepf** (1881m). Carry on along the old alpine path to **Plangäu** (1654m) from where a road leads to Iseltwald. Go across the Plangäugraben downhill as far as Schwand and northwards mostly through forest and across the clearings Point 1297m and Uti onto **Schweibenalp**. Descend the Giessbach gorge down to the **Grandhotel Giessbach** (666m), first on the left, then on the right of the waterfalls. Finally continue on foot or with the venerable funicular railway to the **boat quay** on the Brienzersee.

27 Reeti, 2757m

The Faulhorn actually stands in the shadow of the Reeti

Grindelwald – Holewang – Hireleni-Sattel – Reeti – Bachsee – Waldspitz – Grindelwald

Starting point and destination: Grindelwald (1034m); see Walk 20.
Walking times: ascent 5½ hrs., descent 4 hrs.; total time 9½ hrs.
Difference in height: ascent and descent both 1720m.
Grade: sure-footedness and a lack of vertigo essential in every case, also a certain

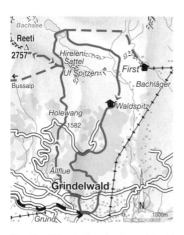

amount of fitness for the way from and to Grindelwald. The upper 350 vertical metres are steep and really exposed and the path is not marked at this point.
Best season: June to October.
Eating place: Restaurant Ällflue.
Accommodation: Berghaus Waldspitz, 30 beds, ✆ 033 853 18 61.
Things to look out for: Grindelwald away from the mountain railway and almost away from the (goods-) roads – a discovery which is worth the effort for this first class viewing summit.
Map: 254 T Interlaken; 1229 Grindelwald.
Alternative: as a detour from the high mountain path 2200 from the cable car mountain station at First (2166m) to the bus terminus at Bussalp (1798m): 5 hrs., ascent 600m, descent 950m. Bus from Waldspitz to Grindelwald station.
Linking walks: 20, 24, 25.
Tip: sit on the north side of the train on the outward and return journey – the view through the window of Reeti produces either disheartening or inspiring emotions. Heimatmuseum in Grindelwald; open Feb. to March (Tue., Fr. 15.00 -18.00) and June to Sept. (Tue., Thurs., Sat., Sun. 10.30-12.00, 15.00-18.00), ✆ 03385343 02.

The Reeti lies in the shadow of the Faulhorn according to the number of visitors. As regards altitude and location, however, the Rötihorn (as it was previously called) stands nearer to the sun than the Faulhorn. Only there isn't a classic hotel on the top of this broken rock, situated a good 1700 metres directly above Grindelwald station, as there is on the Faulhorn and only a narrow path leads onto its exposed summit.
From **Grindelwald** station go westwards along the road in the direction of Bussalp, then right onto a hiking path up to the terraced path. Follow this road for a short way left, then take a little road on the right which leads up to a crossroads of hiking paths (Point 1164m). The direct ascent now begins to the Hireleni col. The marked path runs at first through basin-like forest

Pyramids on the horizon – Wetterhorn and Schreckhorn (right) from the southeast ridge of Reeti. The grassy summit in the foreground is Uf Spitzen.

clearings, later across open slopes northwards past the alpine settlements of **Holewang** (1582m), Spillmatten and Flesch and eventually reaches **Hireleni col** (2327m). The narrow path follows more or less the edge of the southeast ridge, but goes round the pre-summit on the right in the scree. From the next col go up on tracks across scree-covered slabs on the right of the ridge to the top of **Reeti**.

Descend back to the **Hireleni col**. Now go northwards to the **Bachsee** (2265m), up the valley and down the valley to Bachläger and along the roadway to **Waldspitz** (1903m). Continue for a short way along the roadway, then keeping left along the hiking path, descend towards Nodhalten. Shortly before you join the road for the second time, at an altitude of 1660m, at the bottom of the slope, you come to Choleweiher (no name on the map) on the right of the path. Go westwards along the roadway to a crossroads (Point 1620m). Continue in the wood through Strahlgässli to the Restaurant **Ällflue** (1429m). Going southeast through a wood you come to the uppermost houses of Grindelwald. Eventually the Oberhaus/Bim obre Hüs path brings you to **Grindelwald** station.

28 Blau Gletscherli, 2704m

The back side of Grindelwald: silent, stony and quite wonderful

First – Hagelseeli – Hiendertellti – Häxeseeli – Wart – Hornseeli – Grosse Scheidegg

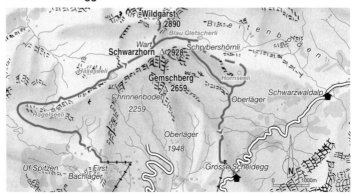

Location: Grindelwald (1034m); see Walk 24.

Starting point: First (2166m), mountain station of the cable car; see Walk 24.

Destination: Grosse Scheidegg (1962m); postbus to Grindelwald or Meiringen; see Walk 30.

Walking times: First – Hagelseeli 1½ hrs., Hagel-seeli – Wart 1½ hrs., Wart – Hornseeli 1¼ hrs., Hornseeli – Grosse Scheidegg 45mins.; total time 5 hrs.

Difference in height: ascent about 900m, descent about 1100m.

Grade: mountain walk along little used paths which are for the most part waymarked, but which hardly exist in places. Route finding necessary. Tricky in fog.

Best season: July to October.

Eating places and accommodation:

First: see Walk 25; Grosse Scheidegg: see Walk 30.

Things to look out for: ice-covered mountains as a backdrop, icebergs in the shadowy lakes.

Map: 254 T Interlaken; 1209 Brienz, 1229 Grindelwald.

Alternative: experienced mountain walkers with a head for heights can ascend Schrybershörnli (2517m) without paths from the north; some rocks at the very top. Afterwards go southeast following the edge of a sheer drop and over the rock belt east Point 2402m keeping left across exposed grassy ledges. Across grassy slopes directly down to Hornseeli.

Linking walks: 24, 25, 29, 30.

Tip: summit seekers can climb from Wart in just under 30 mins. onto Wildgärst (2890m).

Blau Gletscherli: a name full of promise but which hardly comes up to expectations – scree-covered névé that has narrowly survived the greenhouse effect of the 90s. Inspite of this it's very icy on this walk on the shady exterior of the Grindelwald valley basin: both of the cirque lakes Hagelseeli and

Névé and rock – the freshly covered Blau Gletscherli with the Engelhörner.

Häxeseeli are sometimes half frozen over into summer. Together with the sombre Schwarzhorn they contribute to the fact that the landscape in the Hiendertellti and the Hühnertal reminds you of the Rocky Mountains. And then you turn round the corner and the Wetterhorn and Schreckhorn opposite characterize the scenery again. If you want to see these peaks as a mirror image, make a detour to Hornseeli on this remote lake walk.

From **First** go along the beaten path in the direction of Faulhorn as far as a junction just before the Bachsee. Go on the narrow path right to the small lake and through a little valley up onto a col (2416m). On the other side the path descends to **Hagelseeli** (2339m), climbs up onto a rib and drops down into **Hiendertellti**. Continue along here to **Häxeseeli** (2464m) and along a broad ridge up into the **Wart** pass (2704m) between the Schwarzhorn and Wildgärst. Tracks go round the bleak **Blau Gletscherli** on the north side across scree slopes. Descend into the basin below Schrybershörnli. The poor path descends steeply along the Geissbach into Wischbäch valley. Where the ground levels out (at about 2000m) head over left without paths to the hiking path which comes over from Alp Oberläger. Follow this in a cleft up to **Hornseeli** (2147m). Descend to **Oberläger** (1950m) and the roadway via **Gratschärem** (2006m) brings you onto **Grosse Scheidegg** (1962m).

29 Schwarzhorn, 2927m

Highest balcony seat for the awesome sight of Grindelwald's ice mountains

(Grindelwald) – First – via ferrata – Schwarzhorn – Grosse Scheidegg

Location: Grindelwald (1034m); see Walk 24.

Starting point: First (2166m), mountain station of the cable car; see Walk 24.

Destination: Grosse Scheidegg (1962m); bus to Grindelwald or Meiringen; see Walk 30.

Walking times: ascent 3 hrs., descent 2¼ hrs.; total time 5¼ hrs.

Difference in height: ascent 850m, descent 1050m.

Grade: only for skilled mountain hikers; marked path, but exposed and steep path in places in the upper region. Appropriate equipment essential for the via ferrata which is graded easy (harness, karabiners, rope, helmet).

Best season: June to October.

Eating/accommodation: First: see Walk 25; Grosse Scheidegg: see Walk 30.

Map: 254 T Interlaken; 1209 Brienz, 1229 Grindelwald.

Alternative: from Grosse Scheidegg on foot to Grindelwald or Meiringen; see Walk 30.

Tip: guided via ferrata trip with Grindelwald-Sport, ✆ 033 854 12 90; Equipment can be rented.

Linking walks: 24, 28, 30.

This easy via ferrata onto the Schwarzhorn has belonged to the alpine playground of Grindelwald since 1996.

The highest peak to the north of Grindelwald is the Schwarzhorn, 73 metres short of qualifying as a 3000er. It has all the qualities of one of the big hiking summits, but it is not easy to climb. If you are not sure-footed you can easily become intimidated on the steep final section. This is particularly the case for the via ferrata along the southwest ridge which was put up in summer 1996 where there are cables and rungs to help you over the broken rocks on the ascent to the Grosse Chrine (2635m) at the foot of the southwest ridge. Three metal ladders all with 30 rungs surmount the vertical elevations: cables make safe other sections of the climb which is graded easy overall. A little scree path finally leads to the highest viewpoint.

Descend from **First mountain station** and along the upper high mountain path in the direction of Grosse Scheidegg. Turn off left on the Distelboden and go up onto **Chrinnenboden**. Ascend the path across the southwest flank of the Schwarzhorn until the white-blue-white marked via ferrata turns off left. Go into the **Grossi Chrinne** cleft (2635m) and along the protected southwest ridge up onto **Schwarzhorn**. Descend along the sometimes narrow and rocky south ridge onto a broad shoulder. Go northwards onto the southwest flank of the mountain to the ascent route and down onto **Chrinnenboden**. Now along the path east of the Schilt ridge to directly above Alp Oberläger. At the point where you meet the high mountain path follow this over the Gratschärem col onto **Grosse Scheidegg**.

Haslital: mule tracks and reservoirs

'I will tell you nothing of that dreadful path called Helleblatte which has been cut out of hard granite, the same rock as all these mountains, above a terrifying precipice. As we went along it we were met by a large group of pack horses and donkeys which took up the whole width of the road with their loads and it would have been impossible for us to go past them' wrote Jakob Samuel Wyttenbach in his report '*Reise durch die Alpen und das Wallisland*' (Journey through the Alps and the Valais) which came out in 1777. He undertook this journey in the summer of 1771 which led him through the Haslital and over the Grimsel pass into the Rhône valley.

More than 230 years after Wyttenbach had published in 1777 the first (hiking) guide to the Bernese Oberland (compare Walk 18), we are sitting in the post bus Meiringen-Grimselpass-Oberwald; we had reserved the seats by telephone. 'The Sonnenlochtunnel is up ahead which is lit by solar energy', says the driver as we drove along the lowest reservoir of the Oberhasli KWO power station, the Räterichsbodensee. 'Above the tunnel entrance you will see the power lines and to the left of them the solar panels.' Here you become aware of the energy from the sun, the electricity produced from the water in the reservoir, the roar from the car engines and the pipes for natural gas between Holland-Italy below the rugged granite landscape of the Haslital. Tourists are stunned by the grandiose effect of nature in spite of all the concrete walls, cable car cables and power lines, and cyclists puff and pant towards the Valais. For centuries the columns of mules used to bring the hard cheese (Sbrinz) and cattle from the Bernese Oberland and central Switzerland over the Grimselpass and the Griesspass in order to return with wine and rice. The only thing the mule drivers did not export was chocolate. However, they were to find themselves out of work in 1882 with the opening of the Gotthardbahn.

There has been a 'Schoggitaler campaign' in Switzerland every year since 1946: golden medallions (Taler = coin) filled with genuine Swiss chocolate, ensure for posterity an intact landscape. Without these charity campaigns by the Swiss home defence and the Swiss organisation for the protection of nature, the Oberengadiner area of lakes would have been overdeveloped. The 'Schoggitaler' of 1993 helped to make bridges and paths accessible to the public again after they were forgotten and threatened with eventual decay. The mule path over the Grimsel was one path chosen for restoration. It was still well-preserved in several places, between Handegg and Räterichsboden for example, where the Hälenplatte (Walk 34) is to be found. But between Innertkirchen and Guttannen the mule path had been left in a poor condition. 'The Schoggitaler Sale is now to be instrumental towards rebuilding this old section and reactivating it as a hiking path', said the IVS-Bulletin 2/93. The opening took place in the summer 1995 and the

Haslital has gained a very interesting (hiking) path (Walk 33). The whole Grimsel mule path was subsequently repaired from Meiringen to Oberwald, in as far as roads and power stations had not caused its total disappearance.

Another historic path leads over Grosse Scheidegg (Walk 30), at Wyttenbach's time a must for Oberland tourists like the Aareschlucht is today (Walk 31). The Unteraar glacier is also full of history. One of the first to explore this area was the Solothurner scientist Franz Josef Hugi in 1827 (compare Walk 16). You are reminded of Hugi on the Hugisattel on the highest peak of the Bernese Alps, the Finsteraarhorn (4273m), as well as the Hugihornin massif which divides the Lauteraar glacier from the Finsteraar glacier. 'I advise anyone who has an interest in nature in the highest mountains to climb onto the Lauteraar glacier,' wrote Johann Gottfried Ebel in his 'Anleitung auf die nützlichste and genussvollste Art in der Schweitz zu reisen', published in 1793 and translated into English in 1818 'The traveller's guide through Switzerland'. This piece of advice was especially relevant at the end of the 20th century. The KWO wanted to build the gigantic reservoir Grimsel-West. But then their appeal, on a metal board hanging by the tunnel on the Lauteraar hut path (Walk 36), would have been set in concrete as a lie: 'The area around the Grimsel reservoir has been placed under protection as a natural monument on the decision of the canton government. Protect plants and animals!'

Once the steps for mule drivers, but today for hikers – Hälenplatte on the Grimsel pass.

30 Grosse Scheidegg, 1962m

Classic walk over the pass which has been made a right of way again since 1995

Meiringen – Reichenbachfälle – Rosenlaui – Schwarzwaldalp – Grosse Scheidegg – Stepfihubel – Grindelwald

Starting point: Meiringen (595m); see Walk 32.
Destination: Grindelwald (1034m); see Walk 20.
Walking times: Meiringen – Rosenlaui 3 hrs., Rosenlaui – Schwarzwaldalp 30 mins., Schwarzwaldalp – Grosse Scheidegg 1¾ hrs., Grosse Scheidegg – Grindelwald 2½ hrs.; total time 7¾ hrs.
Difference in height: ascent 1370m, descent 930m.
Grade: easy, long, waymarked.
Best season: May to November.
Eating/accommodation: in Meiringen and Grindelwald. Gasthaus Zwirgi (☎ 033 9711422). Gasthaus Kaltenbrunnen-Säge

(☎ 033 9711908). Hotel Rosenlaui (☎ 033 9712912). Berghotel Schwarzwaldalp (☎ 0339713515). Berghotel Große Scheidegg (☎ 033 853 6716).
Things to look out for: cheese stores in the Rosenlauital; one of them dates from 1637.
Map: 254 T Interlaken, 255 T Sustenpass; 1209 Brienz, 1210 Innertkirchen, 1229 Grindelwald.
Alternatives: bus connection [470.65/ 312.20] Meiringen-Grindelwald, change buses on the Schwarzwaldalp (runs June to October). Descent via Hotel Wetterhorn.
Linking walks: 20-22, 28, 29, 31, 32, 45.
Tip: Rosenlaui glacier gorge, open June to October, 45min. trip.

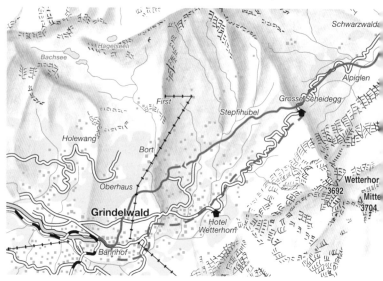

'The journey over this mountain is very interesting because you are close to the high, bare rocky peaks and several glaciers all the time and pretty well always see or hear the most spectacular avalanches. The path is not in the least bit dangerous as it runs the whole way across meadows.' In his 1793 travel guide '*Anleitung auf die nützlichste and genussvollste Art in der Schweitz zu reisen*', this is how the German born and Swiss nationalised Johann Gottfried Ebel described the then fashionable crossing of Grosse Scheidegg (usually from Grindelwald to Meiringen, although the reverse direction offers more dramatic views of the Wetterhorn and Eiger). The first complete travel guide for Switzerland saw several editions and it is still readable today, for Ebel is able to sketch the character and quality of a route with a few strokes (tourists once used to walk!). And since 1995, what he said about the Grosse Scheidegg was right – walkers are no longer endangered by passing cars as was the case for a long time between Willigen and Schwarzwaldalp.

From **Meiringen** station as in Walk 32 go past the Reichenbachfälle or along the old Scheidegg path to **Zwirgi** (971m). The hiking path, opened in 1995, runs along beside the road, over Kaltenbrunnen-Säge (about 1210m, not named on the map) to **Gschwantenmad** (1303m), then on the section officially opened in 1994 to **Rosenlaui** (1328m), up to the entrance to the gorge and south of the pass road along the hiking path onto **Schwarzwaldalp** (1456m). From the Berghotel go back across the Rychenbach again and up the valley across Teiffenmatten to Alpiglen. The hiking path crosses over the road several times and leads directly onto **Grosse Scheidegg**.

Follow the path westwards down to the **Stepfihubel**, along the gorge of the Bärgelbach and eventually across it. Cross over the Horbach. Continue via Point 1458.5m, Schwarzigenhiisren, Hohstand and Oberhaus/Bim obren Hüs to **Grindelwald**, where possible avoiding tarmac roads.

On the right: the Eiger with Mittellegigrat (left) dominates the scenery on the second half of the walk.

Below: Scheidegg-Wetterhorn in profile.

31 Dossenhütte, 2663m

Angry glaciers, ferocious walls, glistening névé, adventurous paths

(Meiringen) – Rosenlaui – Dossenhütte – Urbachtal – Innertkirchen

Location: Meiringen (595m); see Walk 32.
Starting point: Hotel Rosenlaui (1328m) or Gletscherschlucht (about 1360m); postbus [line 470.65] from Meiringen.
Destination: Innertkirchen (625m); see Walk 33.
Walking times: Rosenlaui – Dossenhütte 5 hrs., Dossenhütte – Urbachtal (Mürvorsees) 3½ hrs., Urbachtal –

Alpine route – only for vertigo-free hikers.

Innertkirchen 1 hr.; total time 9½ hrs.
Difference in height: ascent 1340m, descent 2040m.
Grade: for really sure-footed mountain walkers with a head for heights; the path out of the Rosenlauital is in places more of a proteted climbing route. Waymarked as an alpine route with white-blue-white.
Best season: July to Sept. The military is sometimes in the Urbachtal in autumn.
Eating/accommodation: Hotel Rosenlaui; see Walk 30. Dossenhütte SAC, 55 places, always open, staffed from July to September, ✆ 0339 714494. Hotels in Innertkirchen.
Things to watch out for: the huts clinging onto a ridge as if suspended between heaven and earth. The Engelhörner which drop down into the Urbachtal.
Map: 254 T Interlaken, 255 T Sustenpass; 1210 Innertkirchen, 1229 Grindelwald, 1230 Guttannen.
Linking walks: 30, 32, 33, 38, 41.

'The path from here into the Urbachtal is the steepest and most tiring goat path that I know,' recorded Edouard Desor in his book *'Geological Alpine Journeys by Agassiz and his Friends in Switzerland, Savoy and Piemont'*, in which he described the ascent of the Dossenhorn (3138m), amongst others, in the summer of 1843. 'If it's worth paying attention when scrambling down a steep peak so that all obstacles are problems to be overcome, then as soon as you find an easier way, you must not become complacent and thereby run the greater risk.' What would Desor, first ascentionist of the Lauteraarhorn, the Rosenhorn and the Ewigschneehorn, have written if he had been acquainted with the even more difficult path out of the Rosenlauital to the Dossenhütte, which of course didn't exist in those days? From Hotel **Rosenlaui** go to the entrance to the Gletscherschlucht. Continue past it on the right, afterwards cross the bridge over the gorge and climb up to 1680m (the same as the path to the Engelhornhütte). Turn off right and go south along a narrow path to the conspicuous ridge of moraine and over this to a steep step of friable rock. Iron rungs, cable and ladders help you up onto a scree terrace (tricky when wet); continue to the left to the Rosenlauibiwak (only open in the ski season). Above that go over a second

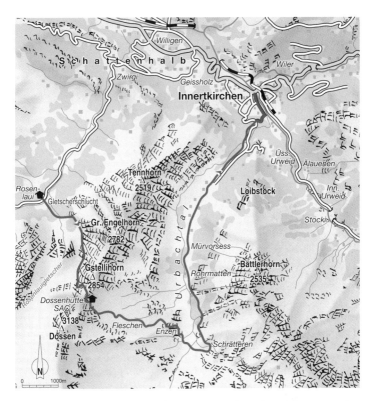

rock step (rungs and cable) and on an exposed section to the connecting ridge Gstellihorn-Dossen and over this to the **Dossenhütte**. From the hut go southwards into a basin often filled with névé and at first eastwards, then south-eastwards over scree, grass and broken rock down to Fleschen. Continue past the ruins of alpine huts onto a shoulder (Point 1879m). Descend the steep path, in places bounded by dense vegetation, across the Alp Enzen (1677m) until, keeping right, you head over towards the Gaulihütte path, on the way crossing over some mountain torrents. This good path is reached above Schrätteren. Follow the right-hand side of the valley to **Mürvorsess** (880m) where the road through the **Urbachtal** begins. Go along this for 3.5 km until the hiking path turns off right up the steep step out of the valley. Follow this path to **Innertkirchen**.

32 Reichenbachfälle and Aareschlucht

Hot on the trail of Sherlock Holmes

Meiringen – Reichenbachfälle – Zwirgi – Geissholz – Aareschlucht – Innertkirchen

Starting point: Meiringen (595m) on the trainline Interlaken-Luzern [470].
Destination: Innertkirchen (625m); see Walk 33.
Walking times: Meiringen – Zwirgi and Zwirgi – Aareschlucht – Innertkirchen both 1½ hrs.; total time 3 hrs.
Difference in height: ascent 150m, descent 350m.
Grade: none.
Best season: April to Oct. (when the

Aareschlucht is open). Reichenbachfälle cable railway in service from middle of May to the middle of Sept. Best time in May and June, when the snow is melting. In autumn and winter the Reichenbachfälle cascade down in the heart of in the heart of the mountain and drives the turbines for the power station.
Eating places: Zwirgi, Lammi and the west and east entrances of the Aareschlucht.
Accommodation: hotels and youth hostels in Meiringen and Innertkirchen.
Things to look out for: the force of the water.
Alternatives: from the Kirchet road more or less along the much driven road to the east entrance of the Aareschlucht and back to Meiringen.
Map: 255 T Sustenpass; 1210 Innertkirchen.
Linking walks: 30, 31, 33, 38, 41.
Tip: Sherlock Holmes Museum in Meiringen with a reconstruction of his living room (open May-Sept. Tue-Thurs 13.30-18.00, October-April Wed-Sun 15.00-18.00).

The brilliant English detective, Sherlock Holmes, lost his life on 4. May 1891 at the Reichenbachfälle of Meiringen when at a dizzy height, he finally intercepted Professor Moriarty, the king of the London underworld. Readers refused to accept the death of their hero in the detective story 'The Final Problem' which is why Conan Doyle had to reincarnate his character in 'The empty house'. A star on the rock face near the cascading water marks the spot where Sherlock Holmes and his opponent lost their grip and fell to their deaths. We are not told unfortunately whether the detective kept a look-out for dangerous criminals in the Aareschlucht, but the scenery would be a totally fitting venue for a detective story. Since 1888 tourists have walked along the paths, daringly constructed across the vertical walls, into the 1400m long and 200m deep gorge.

From **Meiringen** station go through the village and down to the Aare. Shortly after the bridge go right to the valley station and take the funicular railway up to the **Reichenbachfall**. If the cable railway is no longer running, use the hiking path onto Grosse Scheidegg which turns off in Willigen from the main road and leads on the east side of the Reichenbach up to Zwirgi. At the height of the waterfall, a path leads off to a viewpoint. From the mountain station (843m) go up through the basin into which the uppermost Reichenbach waterfall plunges down 75m (the roar of another two waterfalls can be heard below). Cross over the Reichenbach above and you come to **Zwirgi** (971 m). The hiking path to the hamlet of **Geissholz** starts below the inn. Continue northwards to the much used road over the Kirchet pass which you reach at Lammiboden Point 694m. Go north-westwards through the forest down to the Aare at Sandey. Walk to the right to the west entrance of the **Aareschlucht**. Go through the gorge and from the east entrance descend steeply for a short way to the banks of the Aare and up stream to **Innertkirchen**, or go immediately over a footbridge to the Aareschlucht West train stop hidden in the rock.

Aareschlucht with footbridge – another possible location for a detective story.

33 Grimsel mule path

Along the restored section of the old path

Innertkirchen – Boden – Guttannen

Starting point: Innertkirchen (625m); postbus [lines 470.70+71, 470.75+76] or narrow gauge railway [474] from Meiringen.
Destination: Guttannen (1050m). postbus [470.75+76] to Meiringen.
Walking time: 2¼ hrs.
Difference in height: ascent about 450m.
Grade/requirements: none.
Best season: June to October. Early summer is best before the road over the pass is open.
Accommodation: hotels in Innertkirchen. Hotel Urweid on Inneri Urweid (✆ 033 971 26 82). Hotel Adler (✆ 033 973 13 23) and Hotel Bären (✆ 033 973 12 61) in Guttannen.
Things to look out for: four generations of path: route of a medieval mule path, road of 1870, modern road over the pass with tunnels, new standard hiking trail which links together the mule path sections.
Map: 255 T Sustenpass; 1210 Innertkirchen, 1230 Guttannen.
Alternatives: Meiringen – Aareschlucht –

Innertkirchen; 1 hr.; compare Walk 32.
Linking walks: 31, 32, 34, 38, 41.

The Föhn wind has flattened protected forests many times and caused outbreaks of fire as in 1723 and 1803. Avalanches of snow regularly cut off the village of Guttanen from the outside world in winter. Hoards of cars avalanche through the uppermost settlement in the Haslital during weekends in summer. Most of the 400 inhabitants work in the Oberhasli power stations. Like hardly anywhere else in the Bernese Oberland, nature and technology determine the fate of this Bern canton community, more than 200 sq. km. in size. Both co-exist harmoniously on the old mule path between Innertkirchen and Guttannen which was newly opened in 1995 in the Zubenlamm. From the bridge over the Aare in **Innertkirchen** go along the western bank of the Aare up the valley and across two bridges over to the headquarters of the Oberhasli KWO power station (the terminus of the narrow gauge railway is here). Continue along the left-hand side of the road, or a short distance away from it, onto the Üssere Urweid where you cross over the road. The restored mule path lined with dry stone walls leads through meadows and forest up to the pass road. Follow this until the hiking trail again runs a short distance to the side of it. Eventually you cross the road and continue along the restored path over the so-called Zuben, in places almost vertically above the modern road. Descend at the end to the Innere Urweid. At the former inn dating from 1791 cross over the Aare on the bridge which was restored in 1995. Climb up to the Engpass Stocki where the path was hewn out of the rock in 1774 (inscription on the wall). Cross over the mountain pastures to **Boden**. The first Grimsel mule path used to lead on the same side of the valley from here via Ägerstein to Guttannen; this section of the path, however, has not been restored. An earlier mule path (today's hiking trail) crosses onto the other side of the valley and brings you via Flesch and Blindlaui to the Sunnsyten part of **Guttannen**. Inns and a post bus stop can be found on the shady side of the village.

Restored mule path between Üsseren and Zubenlamm.

34 Grimselpass, 2164m

Hot on the trail of mule drivers and poets from the Oberhasli into Obergoms

Guttannen – Handegg – Hospiz – top of the pass – Obergesteln

Starting point: Guttannen (1050m); see Walk 33. From the end of June until the end of September postbus [line 470.75] between Meiringen and Oberwald.

Destination: Obergesteln (1354m) on the bus line [610] Brig-Oberwald-Furka-Andermatt/Göschenen.

Walking times: Guttannen – Handegg 1½ hrs., Handegg – Hospiz 2¼ hrs., Hospiz – top of the pass 45mins., top of the pass – Obergesteln 2½ hrs.; total time 7 hrs.

Height difference: ascent 1160m, descent 850m.

Grade: easy, long, waymarked.

Best season: June to October.

Eating/accommodation: Guttannen;

A power station worker – monument in Handegg.

→ Walk 33. Hotel Handeck (✆ 033 982 66 11). Hotel Grimsel Hospiz (✆ 033 982 66 21). Grimsel pass; compare Walk 35. In Obergesteln: Hotel Grimsel (✆ 027 973 11 56).

Things to look out for: Grimsel cultivated landscape: mule path, old and new pass road, reservoirs, power lines, climbers' lines of bolts.

Map: 255 T Sustenpass, 265 T Nufenenpass; 1230 Guttannen, 1250 Ulrichen.

Alternative: thanks to the postbus you can just do sections of the walk.

Linking walks: 33, 35-39; and Rother Walking Guide to the East Valais.

'From Guttannen onwards the path becomes more and more wild, desolate, unvarying with identically rugged, bleak rocks on both sides. At times you catch sight of a peak which is covered in snow. The ground which is flatter and in some places forms a valley, is strewn with huge boulders. The Aar makes some magnificent waterfalls. Above one of these a daring bridge has been blasted on which you are soaked by the spray'. This is an excerpt from a book by the philosopher Friedrich Hegel, who in the summer of 1796 when he was 26, undertook a 10 day hike through the Bernese Oberland and the Urner Reusstal. Since the Aare flows for the most part through pipes, it no longer forms magnificent waterfalls, but a hike along the path from Guttannen to Obergesteln is worthwhile (it used to be a

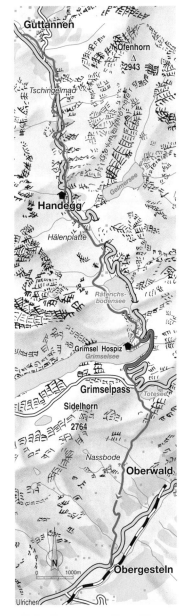

day stage for mule drivers on their way to Italy).

In **Guttannen** cross over the Aare and go up the valley on the east side of the Haslital. At Tschingelmad you come to the pass road. Follow this on the hiking trail to the Handegg headquarters of the power station and up to Hotel **Handegg** (1401m). Now begins the most spectacular section of the Grimsel mule path. Go past the enormous Säumerstein (resting point for mule drivers when they used to transport goods over the mountain) to the Hälenplatte with 16 steps that have been cut into the smooth granite and an inscription by Agassiz, the glacier scientist. Continue along the well-preserved mule path over the small and big Bögelisbrüggli to the **Räterichsbodensee**. The new path, blasted out of the slabs, runs along beside the reservoir. Go through a narrowing to the pass road; leave this after the first hairpin bend and ascend directly and steeply up to the approach road for the new **Grimsel Hospiz** (about 1960m). The historic one sank when the reservoir flooded. Return to the main road and continue along this until you reach the first hairpin bend and go up along the mule path to the **Grimselpass**. Go past the Totesee on its western side. The mule path goes through the glacier-shaped landscape via Point 2205 to Nassbode and descends diagonally the sunny slopes of Grimsle, crossing and using an alpine meadow road, into the village of **Obergesteln**.

35 Sidelhorn, 2764m

Corner point of the Bernese Alps and memorial between Haslital and Goms

Grimselpass – Huseghütte – Sidelhorn

Starting point and destination: Grimsel, top of the pass (2164m); see Walk 34.
Walking times: ascent 1¾ hrs., descent 1¼ hrs.; total time 3 hrs.
Difference in height: 600m.
Grade: easy mountain walk; marked, often stony path, the upper section through rough boulders.
Best season: July to October.
Eating/accommodation: Hotel Grimsel (top of the pass, convenient bunkhouse) (✆ 033 9731137), Grimsel-Blick (✆ 033 9731177), Alpenrösli (✆ 033 973 1291). Berghaus Oberaar (✆ 033 98266 31).

Things to look out for: mountains and valleys, glaciers and scree, reservoirs.
Map: 265 T Nufenenpass; 1250 Ulrichen.
Alternatives: along the southwest ridge into a notch, down the north side to the Triebtenseewli and through a little valley to the Berghaus Oberaar (2338m); hitchhike back to the Grimselpass.
Linking walks: 34; and Rother Walking Guide to East Valais.
Info: Grimselverein, Postfach, CH-3860 Meiringen; Feuer in den Alpen, Postfach 669, CH-3900 Brig, ✆ 027 923 61 62; 'Inns Obergoms', CH-3985 Münster.

'Wandert in der Schweiz, solang es sie noch gibt' (go hiking in Switzerland while there is one) was the opening line of a book by Jürg Frischknecht, 1987. Sidelhorn, the eastern corner point of the Bernese Alps on the canton border Bern – Valais is easily accessible with spectacular views and was an important summit relating to economic policy for two reasons. Firstly, there was a project by unscrupulous tourist planners to develop the Sidelhorn from the Goms onwards with cable cars and ski lifts. And secondly, profit-seeking power station engineers planned to build a huge dam into the existing Grimsel reservoir (Grimsel West) which would ruin the unique landscape of the Unteraargletscher. For this reason the Grimsel festival takes place every year on the second Sunday in August. At the same time memorial fires burn on Sidelhorn and other places in the Alps to help promote their protection from further destruction.

From the western edge of the **Grimsel pass** go along the road in the direction of Oberaar, until the hiking path turns off left. It winds up between granite slabs

Prayer flags in an endangered landscape – celebrations on the Sidelhorn.

and grassy ledges to the closed **Husegghütte**, reaches a ridge and follows this to the summit slope which consists of boulders. Climb up steeply to the highest point of the **Sidelhorn**. Descend the same way as in the ascent.

36 Lauteraarhütte, 2392m

Contrasting fascinations of nature and technology in the largest Bernese nature reserve

Grimsel Hospiz – Grimselsee – Unteraargletscher – Lauteraarhütte

Location: Guttannen (1050m); see Walk 34.

Starting point and destination: Grimsel Hospiz (1962m) just a bit to the west of the road over the Grimsel pass; see Walk 34.

Walking times: outward path 4 hrs.; return path 3½ hrs.; total time 7½ hrs.

Difference in height: 500m between the lake's reflections and hut (according to the map).

Grade/requirements: not very difficult to fairly difficult mountain walk which demands some fitness, sure-footedness and route finding ability. Good path, but also narrow in places and rather exposed along the Grimselsee. No path on the Unteraargletscher, tracks at the very most over rather difficult scree; isolated, but easily seen crevasses. Route marked throughout, white-blue-white from the end of the lake; but you can still lose your way in poor visibility over the Unteraargletscher.

Best season: July to September (when the postbus is in operation).

Eating/accommodation: Hotel Grimsel Hospiz; see Walk 34. Lauteraarhütte SAC, 50 places, always open, staffed July to September, ℃ 033 973 11 10.

Things to look out for: the very crooked Spittellamm dam, the sunny granite slabs with sports climbers, the high alpine fjord of the artificial Grimselsee, the Arvenwald, the tongue of the Unteraar glacier constantly covered in debris, the peaks of Scheuchzerhorn and Agassizhorn glowing red in the last of the evening sun.

Map: 255 T Sustenpass, 265 T Nufenenpass; 1230 Guttannen, 1250 Ulrichen.

Linking walk: 34.

Tip: torch for the lake tunnel.

Up to 1999 the gigantic reservoir project Grimsel West threatened one of the most beautiful landscapes of the Bernese Oberland – reason enough to walk from the Grimsel Hospiz along today's Grimsel reservoir to the Lauteraarhütte. In 1840-45 some plucky scientists and mountaineers lived nearby in the 'Hôtel des Neuchâtelois', a very basic stone hut on the Unteraargletscher. If you take two days over this walk you will spend an unforgettable night at the very heart of the high mountains.

Cultivated landscape of a unique kind – descent to the Spitallamm dam.

From the large car park in front of Hotel **Grimsel Hospiz** go down some steps onto the Spitellammsperre. Go across this, then along a secured path sweeping round to the right up to an unlit tunnel. Through this continue along the partly narrow, but always well-made and visible path in a constant up-and-down along the northern shore of the **Grimselsee** to its end. The now stony path runs over a moraine on the right beside the **Unter-aargletscher** which is covered in debris and boulders, to then reach it at a suitable place. Cross this 'stone-wasteland' without paths following the white-blue-white waymarker posts until a signpost after about 40 mins. at a height of about 2040m bids you leave the glacier again. The moraine path goes along the side of the valley at first really steeply diagonally uphill. After crossing a stream the path leads easily through the grass and granite land-scape to the **Lauteraarhütte**.

Box seat – Lauteraarhütte with the Finsteraarhorn (in the background) and the Agassizhorn to the right of it.

Refreshing spot below the Lauteraarhütte – mountain stream with waymarker.

37 Ofenhorn, 2943m

Very challenging mountain walk onto a relatively empty mountain viewpoint

Chüenzentennlen – Gelmersee – Gelmerhütte – Obrists Diechter – Ofenhorn

Location: Guttannen (1050m) in the Haslital.
Starting point and destination: Chünzentennlen (1596m) on the road over the Grimselpass. Postbus [470.75] from Meiringen via Guttannen or from Oberwald over the Grimselpass; operates from

the end of June to the end of September.
Walking times: Chüenzentennlen – Gelmerhütte and hut – Ofenhorn both 3 hrs., summit – hut and descent to the Grimsel road both 2 hrs. total time 10 hrs.
Difference in height: ascent and descent both 1350m.
Grade: this is not a high mountain trail, but route finding over pathless terrain and confidence with sections of scrambling are necessary. Ice axe an advantage.
Best season: July (hard-packed snow makes the ascent and the descent in the upper section easier) to September. Dangerous if there's snow on the path in the granit slabs above the Gelmersee.
Eating/accommodation: Hotels in Handegg and Grimsel Hospiz; compare Walk 34. Gelmerhütte SAC, 55 places, always open, staffed from July to September, ℃ 033 973 11 80.
Things to look out for: dizzying views down into the Haslital.
Map: 255 T Sustenpass; 1230 Guttannen.
Alternatives: only as far as Gelmersee (graded blue), as far as the hut (red).
Linking walk: 34.
Tip: from the Handegg with the steepest funicular in Europe (up to 106% incline) to the Gelmersee; middle of June to October, daily 9.00-16.00.

The Ofenhorn lies north of the Gelmerhörner, once frequently visited mountains on the eastern side of the Bernese Grimsel pass. The crossing of the mountain, almost a 3000er, from north to south with or without an overnight stop in the modern, cosy Gelmerhütte of the Swiss Alpine Club results in a high trail in a landscape of half tamed, half unspoilt primary rock, part of the Urner Alps but still belonging to the Bernese Oberland and the canton of Bern.

From **Chüenzentennlen** go northwards along the marked path to the Stockseewli and continue in the same direction to the **Gelmersee** (1849m). Cross the dam and keep on the north bank along a path which has been

Rock and névé – Diechterbach above the Gelmer reservoir.

blasted out of the rock in places. Continue in a northerly direction following the path over scree slopes as far as the **Gelmerhütte** (2412m). Beyond the hut take a scree path which runs easily uphill to the north. At the first hairpin bend choose the left-hand turn-off which leads downhill onto the **Obrists Diechter** alluvial plain (about 2390m). Now ascend without paths along the western arm of the Diechterbach. Past a scree-dammed lake and across fields of névé and some boulders you reach a col, marked on the map as 2822m, northeast of the Ofenhorn. Go along the northeast ridge up to the pre-summit (Point 2934m) where tracks alternate with easy scrambling. You can get round a steep reddish rise on the first third of the ridge on the south side. From the pre-summit go along the ridge to the main summit of the **Ofenhorn** which is climbed directly over a few rock steps. Return to the col between the main and pre-summit. Go westwards over boulders down to a field of névé and then in a southerly direction to the Üsseri Garwydilimi crossing (2685m). Now go eastwards across flat scree slopes to reach the ascent route. On the descent from the hut you can also take the unmarked, partly interrupted path on the southern shore of the Gelmersee (more difficult than the normal path).

38 Wannisbordsee, 2103m – Bänzlauialp

Haslital as it has almost always been

Guttannen – Holzhüs – Wannisbordsee – Bänzlauialp – Innertkirchen

Atmospheric moorland plain Obers Hohmad – gap in the clouds for the Bänzlauistock.

Starting point: Guttannen (1050m); see Walk 33.
Destination: Innertkirchen (625m); see Walk 33.
Walking times: Guttannen – Holzhüs 2½ hrs., Holzhüs – Wannisbordsee 45mins., Wannisbordsee – Bänzlauialp 1¼ hrs., Bänzlauialp – Innertkirchen 3½ hrs.; total time 8 hrs.
Difference in height: ascent 1310m, descent 1740m.
Grade/requirements: fitness, sure-footedness and route finding; marked paths, but in the upper section sometimes unclear and not always easy to walk along.
Best season: June to October.
Eating/accommodation: in Guttannen

and Innertkirchen; see Walk 33.
Things to look out for: untamed nature, jagged horizons, bold paths.
Map: 255 T Sustenpass; 1210 Innertkirchen, 1230 Guttannen.
Alternative: from Obers Homad northwards along a path sometimes marked with cairns to the Unterer Bänzlauiseeli (2177m); along the stream without paths across steep grassy slopes directly down across the precipitous southern hillside onto the Bänzlauialp. Very experienced mountain walkers will still want to climb the Bänzlauistock (2530m).
Linking walks: 31-34, 39, 41.
Tip: pack your swimming things.

It's beautiful how the Wannisbordsee lies embedded in a valley basin aligned exactly to the south, how granite rocks tower up in the west above the green water and how the mighty, but slender triangle of the Ritzhorn rises up on the other side of the valley! You do right to jump into the ice-cold water and then while away some time on the shore ... and yet you need to continue your walk because the path across the Bänzlauialp to Innertkirchen is just as impressive. Not only the path, but also this alpine meadow which is miles away from the valley, is a place to linger.

From the post bus stop in **Guttannen** descend to the bridge over the Aare (1050m). Keep left through the district of Sunnsyten to a fork (Point 1053m). Go northwards along the hiking path to the Hostetbach, along beside this uphill and steeply through the forest to Wysstanni, on the way crossing over the alpine road. Go steeply again up the marked footpath, then along the road to the right. Shortly after the bridge (1665m) over the Hostetbach, the mountain path branches off left and leads up across the Untere Farlaui-Alp to the **Alp Holzhüs** (1931m). Continue up along the path northwards and keep left to the outflow of the Wannisbordsee. Follow the stream to the **Wannisbordsee** (2103m).

Descend again onto the high trail (about 2040m) and along the now narrower, more difficult path westwards, finally through a gully onto the moorland plain Obers Hohmad (at Point 2126m). Cross this to a pool where the hiking trail turns off left, descends through the grassy and stony gully north of Point 2126m to 1900m and then crosses the steep hillside northwards to the **Bänzlauialp** (1844m). The alpine path leads aross the steep southern and then western flanks of the Bänzlauistock with a few noticeable counter-ascents to the **Alp Blatten** (1615m). Descend steeply across Ahorni to Älauenen, then along a path beside the stream to Zuben where you come to the historic Grimsel mule path. As in Walk 33 to **Innertkirchen**.

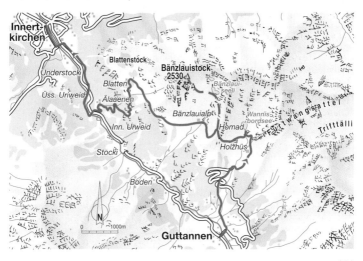

Gadmertal and Hasliberg: alpine pastures and jagged ridges

'The jagged rocks of the Wendenstöcke have towered above the Gadmertal from time immemorial.' This is how the local extreme climber Kaspar Ochsner begins his article which appeared in 1990 in the Munich *'Bergsteiger'* magazine and described climbing on the perpendicular rock faces between Tällistock and Titlis. The Wendenstöcke stand high above the Gadmertal which connects the Sustenpass with the Urner Meiental. From the Gental, lying hidden to the north of these, Engelberg can be reached over the Jochpass. Further to the west the Brünigpass eventually forms the third link between central Switzerland and the district of Oberhasli.

Oberhasli, Hasliberg, Haslital or just Hasli – it is difficult to find your way around the various assortment of names. The Oberhasli covers politically the whole of the administrative district, geographically the catchment basin of the Aare as far as the Aareschlucht, in particular the two large valleys Haslital and Gadmertal. The Hasliberg forms the north-western community in the Oberhasli. Here the landscape is not defined by the white jagged peaks of limestone and névé as in the Gadmertal, but by the alpine pastures which provide another lovely foreground for the ice-covered high alps. Beautiful views for the hiker as well as some spectacular paths which have been opened up in recent years.

Due to the building of the road in 1811 and the modern road, the mule path on the Bernese side of the Sustenpass has disintegrated and is overgrown in places and therefore no longer usable. Nowadays you can experience the walk (Walk 41) along the beautifully made slab path, away from the noisy traffic on the main road, as it runs through unspoilt nature with its boisterous streams. Such an occurrence has become rare in the Alps which makes this an all the more pleasant experience. Just how rare can be seen, if not before, at the point where the lively Steinwasser above Gadmen has been stopped by a wall and disappears into a tunnel. All that remains is a fading trickle.

An intact world in the mountains? You must be joking! The few heli-skiers on Steingletscher infuriate the numerous ski mountaineers, who have arrived by car themselves. The neighbouring informative glacier path takes care of the turnover in Restaurant Steingletscher. In the middle ages, the Alpine pasture dairymen had to fight to keep their the fertile meadows on the Engstlealp and Tannalp, while in the Gental (Walk 45) and surrounding area today, farmers, tourists, power suppliers and soldiers get in each other's way. Alpine access roads make the work easier but the walking more difficult. The water from the Gental is collected in pipes for the turbines to produce electric energy. In between the seasons of the meadows and scree slopes the military takes over. It only remains for the iron ore, once extracted

Contrasts on the hiking path – Wendenstöcke from the bench below the Gadenlauisee.

in opencast mining at Planplatten, to be transported down through the Gental to the blast furnaces in the Gadmertal. Even the medal for tourism has two sides. We can admire the revered hotel on the Engstlenalp, less so the chair lifts in the Melchsee and Planplatten ski resorts (Walks 46, 47), but we still use them sometimes. Such contradictions do not irritate the fishermen. They sit beside the Engstlensee and fish for Canadian trout. The climbers do not worry either. Anyone who climbs the faces of Wenden has no time for other thoughts. Since the summer of 1993 these walls have also been made accessible to experienced mountain walkers. The Tälli via ferrata (Walk 42), the first real via ferrata in Switzerland, goes up across the vertical wall and was planned by Kaspar Ochsner.

39 Furtwangsattel, 2568m

Hut walk between the Gadmertal and Haslital

Furen – Trift – Windegg huts– Furtwangsattel – Holzhüs – Guttannen

Starting point: Furen (1149m) near Gadmen; see Walk 43.

Destination: Guttannen (1050m); postbus to Meiringen or Oberwald [470.75+76].

Walking times: Furen – Windegg 3½ hrs., Windegg – Furtwang col 2 hrs. Furtwang col – Holzhüs 1¼ hrs., Holzhüs – Guttannen 1¾ hrs.; total time 8½ hrs.

Difference in height: ascent about 1500m, descent about 1600m.

Grade: fitness, sure-footedness and route finding necessary. Marked path, but the north side of the pass covered in scree and in places intermittent.

Best season: July to September.

Eating places: restaurant in Furen.

Accommodation: Windegg huts SAC, 12 + 36 places, always open, staffed from July to September, ✆ 033 975 11 10. In Gadmen and Nessental; compare Walk 41. In Guttannen: see Walk 33.

Things to look out for: the cosy Windegg huts. The shingle-roofed mountain huts of Holzhüs. Trifttälli with the Tälliseeli.

Map: 255 T Sustenpass; 1210 Innertkirchen, 1230 Guttannen.

Alternative: from Holzhüs in 5½ hrs. via Wannisbordsee and Bänzlauialp to Innertkirchen.

Linking walks: 33, 34, 38, 40-43.

'Because a new 110 metre high reservoir Grimsel West is planned on Grimsel, half of the projects in the vicinity have to be located higher. It's good that we can approach the octopus of the Grimsel West from one of its many tentacles.' This is a quote from the book where the TransALPedes pioneers documented their long march from Vienna to Nice in 1992. One of the almost 100 stages of just under 2000km went across the Furtwang col, the only pass you can walk across in the glaciered triangle between the Susten, Grimsel and Furka pass roads. This environment that has been and will be transformed by so-called progress – the building and development of power stations. TransALPedes pointed out the threat to the alpine area and

View from Radlefshorn of the tongue of the Triftgletscher above which the Windegg huts are situated.

if you read *'Alpenglühn'* in the evening sun outside one of the Windegg huts, you will be inspired.

From the postbus stop in **Furen** descend to the south to Gadmerwasser, down the valley towards Schaftelen and steeply up the marked path to Schaftellaui. Now the path runs on the sloping right-hand side of the valley up and down through trenches to **Underi Trift** (1357m), mountain station of a power station cable railway. Cross over the standing water in the pasture. Go up the left-hand side of the valley to the Bosslis Stein where the path forks; right goes to the **Windegg huts** (1887m) which are not visible until the last moment. From there the path climbs southwards onto the Windegg, follows this ridge and runs on the level into Trifttälli to the Tälliseeli (2267m). It's now a tiring climb up onto the **Furtwang col**. The path descends very steeply to a junction (Point 2391m). The right-hand path leads down through the Rindertal and crosses over to **Alp Holzhüs** (1931m). Continue as in Walk 38 to **Guttannen**.

40 Gadenlauisee, 2155m

A quiet mountain lake in which Dolomite-like rock faces are reflected

Gadmen – Hubel – Gadenlauisee – Hubel – Furen

Starting point: Gadmen (1205m); see Walk 43.
Destination: Furen (1149m); see Walk 43.
Walking times: ascent 3½ hrs., descent 2 hrs.; total time 5½ hrs.
Difference in height: ascent and descent both about 1000m.
Grade: short, but not easy mountain walk due to the sometimes overgrown and poorly marked paths.

Best season: July to October.
Eating places: restaurant and grocer's in Furen.
Accommodation: in Gadmen; see Walk 41.
Things to look out for: the white of Scheuchzer's cotton grass and of the sheep. The green of the moss, ferns and the granite.
Map: 255 T Sustenpass; 1210 Innertkirchen.
Alternative: from the eastern shore of the lake southwards across grassy ribs onto moraine and finally over a névé slope into a notch (2501m). Shorter descent through a gully of friable rock, crossing of scree slopes and the steep southeastern hillside over grassy ledges onto the Radlefshorn (2603m); 1½ hrs. from the Gadenlauisee, only for mountain walkers.
Linking walks: 39, 41-43.
Tip: ski sticks are useful on the narrow fern-covered paths.

'This magnificent mountain lake with its clear emerald green mirror situated at an altitude of about 2100m is well worth a visit', enthused Albert Hürner in his book 'Wanderbilder aus dem Gadmertal' (Pictures of walks through the Gadmertal) from 1910. In fact, if the vertical walls of the Tällistock-Titlis chain of mountains are reflected in the still Gadenlauisee, then it is a sight as splendid as the Bachsee with the Grindelwaldner ice mountains, for example. However in the Gadmertal, there are far fewer tourists, which means that you can enjoy the bilberries all on you own on the adventurous descent to Furen.

From **Gadmen** go southwards through the village down to the bridge over Gadmerwasser and up onto a forestry road. Continue along the hiking path which follows a laid service road and is interrupted by this in places, then winds up through the dark Farlaui forest to the alpine mountain huts of **Hubel** (1854m). The path follows a ridge over grassy granite steps southwards up to the **Gadenlauisee**. Return along the same path to **Hubel**, but now descend the path through dense vegetation across the hillside down the valley. Through the Schaftellaui forest to the avalanche line of the same name and along a stream down to the Schaftelen road to **Furen**.

Mirror, mirror on the wall – Wendenstöcke with hiker.

41 Sustenpass, 2250m

To walk where everyone drives – along old mule paths

Sustenpass – Steingletscher – Gadmen – Furen – Nessental – Innertkirchen

Location: Meiringen (595m); see Walk 32. Göschenen (1102m) on the Gotthard [600].
Starting point: top of the Sustenpass (2224m); by postbus [470.70] from Meiringen via Innertkirchen or from Göschenen via Wassen; end of June to the end of Sept.; information, ✆ 033 828 88 28.
Destination: Innertkirchen (625m); see Walk 33.
Walking times: Sustenpass – Steingletscher 45mins., Steingletscher – Gadmen 2 hrs., Gadmen – Nessental 1¼ hrs., Nessental – Innertkirchen 1¼ hrs.; total time 5¼ hrs.
Difference in height: descent 1630m.
Grade: easy, rather long, waymarked; you can break the walk at several postbus stops.

Traffic noise and hard road surface in places.
Best season: June to October.
Eating places: top of the Sustenpass and in Furen.
Accommodation: Hotel Steingletscher (✆ 033 975 12 22). Hotel Alpenrose in Obermad (✆ 033 975 11 55). Hotel Bären in Gadmen ✆ 033 975 12 42). Hotel Tännler in Wiler (✆ 033 971 14 27). Hotels in Innertkirchen.
Map: 255 T Sustenpass; 1210 Innertkirchen, 1211 Meiental.
Alternative: ascent of Wassen (916m) through the Urner Meiental to the top of the pass in 5½ hrs.
Linking walks: 31-33, 38-40, 42, 43.
Tip: walk from Innertkirchen through the Aareschlucht to Meiringen; see Walk 32.

Modelled on the design of old mule paths, a 4.5km long stretch of path on the Bernese side of the Sustenpass was restored in 1992/93 between Steingletscher and Gadmen. This is the quietest section of this exciting walk on the highest road pass in the Oberland.

From the west entrance (2224m) of the apex tunnel on the **Sustenpass** climb to the top of the pass (about 2250m). Return to the postbus stop, fol-

Old and new path on the diagonal – Susten mule path below Sustengletscher.

low the new road for a short way, then turn left onto the route of the 1811 road; crossing the main road twice, it leads down to **Steingletscher** (1865m). Continue along the renovated mule path via Wyssenmad, at first south, then north of Steinwasser until you come to the plain (1220m) east of **Obermad**. Go across the river again and on the left of the Gadmerwasser descend the valley and go past the turn-off for Gadmen (if there's shooting practice, go via **Gadmen**). Continue down the valley along a little road via **Furen** (1131m), Schaftelen and a steep step to the Bidmi bridge. Shortly after that go under the main road to Milistalden and to **Nessental** (925m). Below this cross over the road and the river again; quiet meadow paths lead via Hopflouenen to Schwendi and a little road leads to **Wiler**. Follow the road for a short way here until the hiking path turns off to Bottigen and **Innertkirchen**.

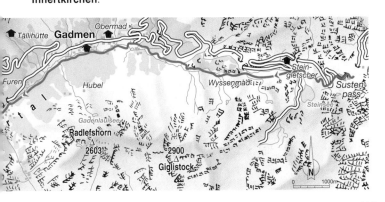

42 Tälli via ferrata, 2540m

Teetering on the abyss: adrenalin rush for experienced mountain walkers

(Sustenpass road) – Tällihütte – Gadmerflue – Gental – Tällihütte or Engstlenalp

Location: Furen (1149m); see Walk 43.
Starting point: Tällihütte (1726m); compare Walk 43; 1½ hrs. from the Sustenpass road.
Destination: Tällihütte (1716m) or Engstlenalp (1834m); see Walk 45.
Walking times: Tällihütte return 7-8 hrs., with descent to Engstlenalp 1 hr. shorter.

Difference in height: ascent and descent both 1000m with return to the Tällihütte; actual via ferrata 500m, with shoulder 600m.
Grade/requirements: moderately difficult, very long via ferrata, in places very exposed. If you are in the least bit uncertain, you would be better to go with a mountain guide.
Equipment: harness, 2 screwgate karabiners with slings, belay device, helmet. The specialized via ferrata gear can be rented in Meiringen, eg. at Pollux-Sport, but you should certainly know how to use the gear.
Best season: July to the beginning of October. There are dangerous patches of old snow in early summer.
Eating/accommodation: Tällihütte, Bergführerverein Haslital, 26 places, open and staffed from mid-June to mid-October, ✆ 033 975 14 10.
Things to look out for: modern preparation of the mountain for tourists.
Map: 255 T Sustenpass; 1210 Innertkirchen.
Linking walks: 39-41, 43-45.
Tip: leaflets from the tourist information. Mountain guide office for the Tälli at Pollux-Sport in Meiringen, ✆ 033 971 43 18.

Situated to the north above the Susten road are vertical limestone walls, 500 to 1500m high, running from Tällistock across the Wendenstöcke as far as Titlis. The middle section is known as Wenden amongst extreme climbers from all over Europe and the western section is marked as Gadmerflue on the map. The via ferrata which was opened in 1993 is to the west of the Horlauipfeiler. Taking 2200 hours of work by volunteers and at a cost of 150,000 francs, members of the Haslital mountain guide organisation drilled 660 holes into the rock, placed 550 iron rungs and 25 stanchions, installed 48 metres of iron ladders, laid 1300 metres of steel cable for the first genuine via ferrata in Switzerland.

From the **Tällihütte** go north-eastwards along white-blue-white marked and finally protected path over visibly more precipitous ground, past the Alpligerstöckli (1912m), to the **Alpligerstock** (2067m) at the foot of the face of Gadmerflue where the actual via ferrata begins. After the breathtaking approach (which has been deliberately chosen to test prospective candidates for the via ferrata), the wall leans back slightly. The path creeps along the break points of the wall, skilfully uses grassy ledges and stepped platforms. There are no escape routes. It is possible to reverse the route but that would be more difficult than going on up. A third of the way up you reach a roomy cave with a wooden bench. Just below the exit from the route you come to another wooden bench in a niche where there's a book in the wall. From the 'summit' of the via ferrata (about 2540m, east Point 2598m) go along the white-blue-white marked trail north-westwards over scree and grass, past Point 2230m, onto the hiking path which you reach at Point 2121m.

As in Walk 43 return to the **Tällihütte** or go on to **Engstlenalp**.

New path on the vertical – approach to the Tälli via ferrata.

43 Sätteli, 2116m

High mountain trail below the Hasli-Dolomites from the Gental into Gadmertal

Engstlenalp – Sätteli – Tällihütte – Furen or Gadmen on the Sustenpass

Starting point: Engstlenalp (1834m); see Walk 45.

Destination: Furen (1149m) or Gadmen (1205m); postbus to Meiringen or to Wassen/Göschenen [line 470.70 +71]. The marked and partly restored path reaches the road over the Sustenpass at Point 1171m, 500m above Furen at the

valley station of the goods cable railway to the Tällihütte; no official postbus stop.

Walking times: Engstlenalp – Sätteli 2¾ hrs., Sätteli – Tällihütte 1 hr., Hütte – Furen 1 hr., hut – Gadmen 1¼ hrs.; total time about 5 hrs.

Difference in height: ascent 300m, descent 1000m.

Grade: marked mountain walk which demands sure-footedness; some exposed places, especially on the descent from the Sätteli (be especially careful when wet).

Best season: July to October.

Eating/accommodation: Engstlenalp; compare Walk 44. Tällihütte; compare Walk 42. In the Gadmertal; compare Walk 41.

Things to look out for: diverse fauna (rare butterflies and adders) and flora (change of damp north side to the dry south side). The Alps threatened by avalanches of stones and snow which cling to the valley slopes on both sides of the Gadmerflue.

Map: 255 T Sustenpass; 1210 Innertkirchen.

Linking walks: 39-42, 44, 45.

Tip: if you do not want to do the Tälli via ferrata you can use descent route onto Gadmerflue; see Walk 42.

'This mountain pasture is not only one of the most beautiful in Switzerland with regard to its views, it is in itself the very model of a Swiss Alp with flower-covered meadows, sturdy fir trees, venerable stone pines, pretty alpine flowers (numerous alpine roses), cascading mountain streams, exquisite spring water (4° C), excellent milk, with a lake to the southeast full of trout whose water temperature rises to 15° C on warm days and where you can also go for a swim.' This is how Theodor Gsell-Fels described the Engstlenalp in 1880. But even lovelier views can be had from the Sätteli, the notch between vertical limestone merlons which are also called the Hasli-Dolomites. Together with views of the western Urner and eastern Bernese Alps, you can also look down into the Gental and Gadmertal.

Approaching the Sätteli across hillsides that seem to go on for ever.

From the **Engstlenalp** go south along the hiking path past the outflow of the **Engstlensee** onto Alp Scharmad. Take the path on the left which is the upper path below the precipices of the Gadmerflue and the Tällistock in an easy up-and-down (and finally up a considerable incline) across mostly steep grass and scree slopes into the **Sätteli** notch (2116m). The path zigzags steeply down across the vertiginous southern hillside and the crosses over to the **Tällihütte** (1726m). The paths divide here. Either take the high trail crossing over several very steep trenches, via Alpligen onto the Alp Raflue (1603m) from where the path runs down towards the Horlauigraben, follows it on its left-hand side and eventually reaches **Gadmen**. Or go from the Tällihütte along the hut path to the Lägerrain car park and before you reach the road, go down left to a section of this road situated much further below. Continue along here to the other side of the Üsser Flüeligraben, then go along a path directly down to the Sustenpass road (Point 1171m). Follow the road to **Furen**.

44 Jochpass, 2207m

A section of the alpine pass trail Sargans-Montreux

Engelberg – Trüebsee – Jochpass – Engstlensee and Engstlenalp

Starting point: Engelberg (1000m); train [line 480] from Luzern.
Destination: Engstlenalp (1834m); see Walk 45.
Walking times: Engelberg – Trüebsee 2¾ hrs., Trüebsee – Jochpass 1¼ hrs., Jochpass – Engstlenalp 1 hr.; total time 5 hrs.
Difference in height: ascent 1200m, descent 370m.
Grade: easy mountain walk along marked paths which need a certain amount of fitness for the ascent or money for the mountain railway.
Best season: July to Oct.; possible snowfields in June on the north side of the Joch-pass. Engelberg cable car – Trüebsee, always runs except for two weeks in Nov. The chair lifts from the Trüebsee onto the Jochpass and beyond towards the Engstlensee also run in the summer.
Eating/accommodation: Hotels and youth hostels in Engelberg. Café Ritz on Vorder Stafel/Gerschnialp (✆ 041 637 22 12), Hotel Trübsee (✆ 041 637 13 71), Berghaus Jochpass (✆ 041 637 11 87). Berghotel Engstlenalp, open from middle June until October, (✆ 033 975 11 61.
Things to look out for: Engelberg monastery. The revolving cabins of the cable

car onto Klein Titlis. The ice cap of Titlis. The limestone towers of the Wendenstöcke. The stone pines in the nature reserve of Engstlensee.
Map: 245 T Stans, 255 T Sustenpass; 1191 Engelberg, 1210 Innertkirchen, 1211 Meiental.
Alternative: ascent by cable cars.
Linking walks: 42, 43, 45.

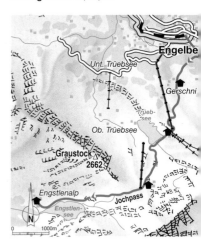

The 1910 year book of the Swiss Ski Organisation says that 'the first skiers to plough through the virgin slopes of the Engelberg were the gentlemen Hans Immer and his companions Melch. Thöni and Joh. Berg. They came in the winters of 1893 and 1894 over the Jochpass to Engelberg'. Follow the trail of these ski pioneers more than100 years later in summer and you will notice almost everywhere that their feat has not been without its consequences. But in spite of the pylons and ski slopes, cables and bars, this landscape right in the middle of the cantons Bern, Obwalden and Nidwalden is still worth visiting thanks to the rock and névé of the nearby peaks.

Visited by skiers for over 100 years – Engstlensee on the edge of the Oberland.

From **Engelberg** station go south-eastwards through the Lindenallee to the bridge over the Engelberger Aa then along a good path over the forested steep step to the high plain of the **Gerschnialp** (Vorder Stafel, 1257m). Continue southwards to the bushy steep slope of Pfaffenwand (Staldi on the map) which is crowned with the **Hotel Trübsee** (1796m) and cable car buildings. Descend to the **Trüebsee** (1764m). After the bridge over the inflow go left and along a path fairly steeply up to the **Jochpass** (2207m); you can also take the path which leads up along beside the chairlift. From the pass descend along the (right-hand) path to the **Engstlensee** (1850m). At this point do not go directly to Berghotel **Engstlenalp** (1834m), choose instead the pretty roundabout route along the northwest shore.

45 Gental

Sunny high mountain trail with shady sections through a little known valley

Engstlenalp – Baumgarten – Schlafenbielen – Reuti – Meiringen

Location and destination: Meiringen (595m) on the train line [470] Interlaken-Luzern.

Starting point: Engstlenalp (1834m); postbus [470.80] from Meiringen; runs from the end of June to mid-October.

Walking times: Engstlenalp – Baumgarten 1 hr., Baumgarten – Moosbielen 1½ hrs., Moosbielen – Reuti 1 hr., Reuti – Meiringen 1 hr.; total time 4½ hrs.

Difference in height: ascent 320m, descent 1560m.

Grade: not a very difficult mountain walk along partly marked paths; now and then sure-footedness an advantage.

Best season: July to October.

Eating/accommodation: Engstlenalp; compare Walk 44. Hotels in Meiringen and Reuti.

Things to look out for: the Wetterhörner at the end of the valley.

Map: 255 T Sustenpass; 1210 Innertkirchen.

Alternatives: from the Engstlenalp via Balmeregghorn and Planplatte in 5¼ hrs. to Reuti (more people, more lifts, more peaks).

Linking walks: 7, 30, 31, 42-44, 47.

Advice: the Muggestutz path of the dwarfs, very popular with children, runs from the Mägisalp to Bidmi (both reachable by cable car) (2 hrs.). Leaflet, book and cassette from Tourist Information Hasliberg.

'The Gental has the classic U-shape of a glaciated valley. The grey walls are steep and rocky and contrast aesthetically with the verdant valley floor' wrote William Reifsnyder in his guide '*Footloose in the Swiss Alps*', published by the Sierra Club in San Francisco in 1974. He described treks in Switzerland and the alpine pass route Sargans-Montreux, called the Hintere Gasse in the Bernese Oberland (compare Walk 50), forms the main part. A stage of this Swiss trail runs through the Gental.

From Berghotel **Engstlenalp** go along the mountain trail, leaving the turn-offs to Tannalp on the right, across the rear south-eastern hillside of the Gental onto **Alp Baumgarten** (1702m). It's an easy climb up out of the valley along a roadway. After 800m the hiking path turns off right. It leads

A rest in front of the Moosbielenhütte with its wooden carvings and concrete floors.

across some fairly steep grassy hillsides onto a shoulder of the Balmeregg, at the edge of the **Wüost** basin embedded into the valley hillside (north of Point 1861 m). Descend into this basin, cross its streams and go along the mountain trail across the steep hillside onto the **Alp Schlafenbielen** (1937m). Follow the little alpine access road to the furthest edge of the

Gental and continue along the old alpine path which descends on the right across a grassy slope to the **Alp Moosbielen** (1621m). Carry on along the road from which the official hiking path turns off left to Reuti. Stay on the road, but shorten the second bend along the old alpine and hiking path (the turn-off is not easily visible!) and descend the path further past Point 1475m to Gwiggi. Descend the little road on the right and cross the Mili stream to the road Reuti-Bidmi until the hiking path turns off right to **Reuti**. The hiking trail to Meiringen begins at the point where you meet the main road Reuti (1061m). Finally go through the village to **Meiringen** station.

46 Gibel, 2035m

Muddy mountain trail, peak with wonderful views, long descent

Meiringen/Hasliberg – Käserstatt – Gibel – Feldmoos – Brünigpass

Location: Meiringen (595m) or Hasliberg-Wasserwendi (1160m); see Walk 47.

Starting point: Käserstatt (1831 m); see Walk 47.

Destination: Brünigpass (1002m); see Walk 1.

Walking times: Käserstatt – Gibel 1¼ hrs., Gibel – Brünigpass 3 hrs.; total time 4¼ hrs.

Difference in height: ascent 200m, descent 1030m.

Grade: trainers not suitable for this walk: sometimes narrow grassy or boggy paths. Otherwise easy and well marked.

Best season: June to October.

Eating/accommodation: Berghaus Käserstatt, ✆ 033 971 27 86. In Meiringen and Hasliberg. Brünigpass; see Walk 1.

Things to look out for: Schwingen (a Swiss traditional kind of wrestling): Brünig-Schwinget every year last Sunday in July, Käserstatt-Schwinget at beginning of Aug. (exact details from the tourist offices). Otherwise: panorama, herds of cows, acorn trees.

Map: 254 T Interlaken, 255 T Sustenpass; 1209 Brienz, 1210 Innertkirchen.

Alternative: ascent of Hasliberg-Hohfluh (1051m) via Gadmen, Balisalp/Vorder Staffel and Steinschlag-Hütte onto Gibel; 2½ hrs. You go past the so-called Berner (Bernese) Gibel southwest of the actual main summit(beautiful view down into the valley, barbecue site). This spot can also be easily reached from the main path.

Linking walks: 1, 45, 47.

Tip: Hasliberger village path, an architectural walk opened in 1993 with 23 characteristic houses and village tableaux on the sun terrace; 3 hrs. Be sure to take with you the informative brochure from the tourist office with the exact location of the houses so that you only see the really beautiful buildings and not the architectural mistakes.

The crossing of the Gibel from Käserstatt to the Brünigpass is a popular walk which is also recommended by the tourist offices of Meiringen and Hasliberg. And rightly so, for the view of Gibel from the ridge is very impressive. The eastern Bernese Alps glisten majestically, the glaciers of the Sustenhorn-Dammastock group gleam alluringly and Basòdino peeps over across the Grimsel. And then there's also the view of the Brienzersee and

Idyllic scenery in the foreground with the Wetterhörner, Mönch and Eiger behind.

the Obwaldner Seenplatte. However, you have to keep your eyes on the path along this high mountain trail which has been rutted by the hooves of cows.

From the cable car mountain station on **Käserstatt** it's a leisurely ascent on the mountain trail across the moderately steep, grassy slopes of Hohbiel and Chingstuel onto Schonegg. Go round Chlyne Gibel on the right-hand side and directly onto **Gibel**. From the summit the path makes a considerable swing round to the left onto Laucherboden and you descend the grassy ridge onto a col (1812m). Go along a little alpine road over the mostly wooded western side until the hiking path turns off left to the Brünig. It makes its way down to Feldmoos. Now – swinging round to the north – continue along a little alpine road again which leads to the acorn trees of Esleren. A hiking path branches off shortly afterwards at a bend. The hiking trail descends alternatively over grass and gravel or even concrete, through meadows and forest, down to the railway track. Follow this then go along the road which brings you in a few minutes to the **Brünigpass**.

47 Hochstollen, 2480m

The short summit walk to the long leave-taking of the Bernese Oberland

Hasliberg – Käserstatt – Hohsträss – Hochstollen – Melchsee-Frutt

The tinkling of cow bells, ice mountains, mountain railways – the Bernese Oberland presents its lively, aesthetic, tourist side again from here. In this part of the Alps you can experience an idyllic, soothing alpine pasture scenery close at hand and the untamed, glaciated, unmistakable mountains beyond, all of which became so irresistible to the first tourists in the 18th century – and so easily accessible.

From **Käserstatt** go north-eastwards up to **Hohsträss**, along the meadow path. From there the good mountain path follows a ridge at first, crosses a grassy valley basin to the crossing of Wit Ris and runs elegantly along the jagged south ridge onto the **Hochstollen** where there's a summit cross and book. Continue along the path on the narrow north ridge down to Abgschütz, to the right into the Tschugglen basin and past the Blausee to the **Melchsee** with a tourist settlement and mountain station of the cable railway.

Typical Bernese Oberland – unmistakable peaks, easily accessible inns.

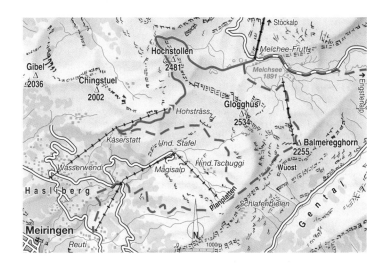

Location: Meiringen (595m) on the train line Interlaken-Brünig-Sarnen-Luzern [470]. Or Hasliberg-Wasserwendi (1160m) above Meiringen; postbus [470.50] from the Brünigpass.

Starting point: Käserstatt (1831 m). Mountain station of the Hasliberg-Wasserwendi cable car; runs from mid-June to the end of October. From Meiringen take the cable railway to Reuti and from there the Hasliberg-postbus to Wasserwendi.

Destination: Melchsee-Frutt (1902m); cable railway (mid-June to the end of October) onto Stöckalp (1075m) and by postbus [470.25] through the Melchtal to Sarnen.

Walking times: Käserstatt – Hohsträss and Hohsträss – Hochstollen both 1 hr., Hochstollen – Melchsee 1½ hrs.; total time 3½ hrs.

Difference in height: ascent 650m, descent 580m.

Grade: take with you a portion of sure-footedness, leave out the vertigo

and add provisions and fitness to taste.

Best season: June to October.

Eating/accommodation: Käserstatt, see Walk 47. In Meiringen, Hasliberg, Melchsee-Frutt.

Things to look out for: Eiger, Mönch and Wetterhörner say good bye as the central Swiss peaks lure you with new walks.

Map: 255 T Sustenpass; 1210 Innertkirchen.

Alternative: from the northeast shore of the Melchsee (1891m) onto Balmeregghorn (2255m). Breathtaking mountain trail to Planplatten / Alpen Tower (2233m). From there three possibilities: by cable cars over the Mägisalp to Reuti; on foot to Käserstatt; descent through the Gummen to Bidmi and on to Reuti or Wasserwendi. Walking time depends on use of mountain railways 1 to 4 hrs.

Linking walks: 43-46.

Tip: from Melchsee in 1½ hrs. via Tannensee and Tannen onto Engstlenalp.

Trekking: 'Dür z'Oberland uuf ...'

'If you can run like a chamois and prefer to stay on the beaten track, and like putting all your health and energy into it, you can experience the very essence of the Oberland in four days although we think it almost a sin to give you a plan.' In his *'Hand Atlas für Reisende in das Berner Oberland'* (Handy atlas for Travellers in the Bernese Oberland) from 1816 Johann Rudolf Wyss gives the following, in those days already classic route: day 1: from Bern by carriage to Thun, by boat to Interlaken and on foot or by small carriage to Lauterbrunnen; day 2: over Kleine Scheidegg on foot to Grindelwald; day 3: over Grosse Scheidegg on foot to Meiringen; day 4: by carriage to Brienz, by boat across the Brienzesee and Thunersee and once more by carriage back to Bern. Today you need two days for the journey through the eastern Bernese Oberland if you plan to cover the same routes as the travellers at that time on foot; and only one day if you use all the trains, busses and boats on the way.

Thanks to the Eiger North Face and the train to the Jungfraujoch, Kleine Scheidegg is still one of the most popular destinations in the Oberland. It forms, then as now, the centre section of a journey on foot through this part of the (Swiss) Alps. The Hintere Gasse, a route from Meiringen which leads over eight passes past the foot of the Eiger, Blümlisalp and Wildstrubel to Gsteig, needs eight days. It can also be done in eight separate instalments since public transport makes all the locations accessible and sometimes the passes as well. But if you can run like a chamois, you will only want to walk along the Hintere Gasse (Walk 50) and the other two multi-day walks in the Oberland introduced here (Walks 48, 49) which run north and south of Thunersee and Brienzersee.

On all three treks you usually stay overnight in the mountains. When, on the fifth day of the summit walk from the Stockhorn to the Faulhorn, you fall into the historic beds of the hotels built in 1830 (the mattresses and bed linen are new!) then it seems as if you are almost one of the first tourists in the Alps who gazed in wonder at the sunset and sunrise here. Of course, you could pack a tent and some food and take a whole week to walk from east to west. But to puff and pant for days with a heavy sack past cosy inns, stylish hotels and delicious bakeries is no fun. So take a small rucksack with you instead and stop and buy some food from the various locations in between. You will certainly be glad of a light pack if you combine the three routes into a three week marathon of Oberland hiking. *'Dür z'Oberland uuf und dür z'Oberland ab'* (Up and Down the Oberland) is the song on your lips. Both the Rother guides in your rucksack lid; that's a good 280 pages. With its 84 pages, the *'Hand Atlas'* by Wyss was the rucksack guide (so the idea of short guides today is not entirely new) to his work in two volumes with 914 pages *'Reise in das Berner Oberland'* of 1816/17, from which I could quote page after page.

From east to west or the reverse – every route goes (went) past the Brienzersee.

For example: 'To have spent a quiet day on a high alp like the Scheideck, in a mountain village like Mürren, in a hostel like the Grimsel, to feel at one with the alpine folk, to watch with a heartfelt empathy for nature the tending of the herds and the full day's work of an Alpine dairyman, to enjoy the morning sun and evening light, the change of light and the effectiveness of the natural powers of a tranquil atmosphere – is to experience the bliss of a totally idyllic world.' Or, even better: Wyss describes the Bernese Oberland peaks as 'ice-laden pillars of heaven which are of such singular beauty and grandeur that their outline on the horizon either outstrips, by their majesty and multiform splendour, even the mountains of Greece and towering Tibet, the Caucasus and the Cordillieren of America or at least seems to match them'.

48 From the Brienzer to the Sigriswiler Rothorn

Twelve peaks north of Brienzersee and Thunersee

Brünigpass – Brienzer Rothorn – Chli Schnierenhörnli – Hohgant – Niederhorn – Sigriswiler Rothorn – Blueme – Thun

Starting point: Brünigpass (1002m) on the train line [470] Interlaken-Luzern.
Destination: Thun (560m) on the train line Interlaken-Zurich.
Walking time: a total of 40 hrs. (90 km).
Difference in height: ascent 6,100m in total, descent 6,600m in total.
Grade/requirements: challenge for fit, sure-footed hikers. Paths usually marked.
Best season: June to October.
Eating/accommodation: Berghotels and country inns.
Food: small shop in Innereriz.
Map: 253 T Gantrisch, 254 T Interlaken.
Alternatives: from Bitschigrind below the Állgäu Lücke descent to Oberried on the Brienzersee (2 Hotels). As 3rd stage via Blasenhubel, Augstmatthorn, Suggiturm and Horetegg to Habkern; 9 hrs. (Walk 4; East). From Habkern via Gemmenalphorn to the Niederhorn; 4¾ hrs. (Walk 47; West).

Strictly speaking, the peaks north above the Brienzersee and Thunersee do not belong to the Bernese Alps but according to a generally accepted German division, to the Emmentaler Alps. Certainly the peaks in the southernmost chain between Brünigpass and Thun are amongst those of the Bernese Oberland which is why they have been included in walking guides to this area. Moreover the peaks between Brienzer and Sigriswiler Rothorn offer the most varied panorama in the whole of the Oberland. The blue lakes lie shimmering directly below with their white boats and the white high alps glisten opposite below a blue sky. And there are contrasts not only in the views. Even the contrast between the solitude along the way and the activity on some of the summits, is striking especially with the day trippers on the Brienzer Rothorn and the Niederhorn. It's just the same when stillness descends in the evening after they have left and the paragliders have also disappeared.

Summit-hungry hikers on the third day on the crossing of Hohgant might venture up onto the Aff after they have already taken in Wilerhorn and Höch Gumme on the first day. Alpinists should follow the whole of the Brienzer ridge from the Brienzer Rothorn to the Harder above Interlaken. Outside the tourist borders at the northern foot of Hohgant lies Kemmeriboden Bad which already belongs to the Emmental. The speciality dessert, for which this country inn is famous throughout the region, is meringues and comes originally from Meiringen in the Bernese Oberland.

The six stages (with walk number and guide book volume):

■ 1. Brünigpass – Arnihaaggen – Brienzer Rothorn; 5¾ hrs. (Walk 1; East);

■ 2. Brienzer Rothorn – Planalp – Állgäu Lücke – Chli Schnierenhörnli –

One of the high points – a view back of the first day's stage from the Brienzer Rothorn.

Kemmeriboden Bad; 7 hrs. (Walk 2; East);

3. Kemmeriboden Bad – Hohgant – Innereriz; 8½ hrs. (Walk 3; East);

4. Inneriz – Grüenenbergpass – Gemmenalphorn – Niederhorn; 6 hrs. (Walks 46, 47; West);

5. Niederhorn – Beatenberg – Justistal – Sigriswiler Rothorn – Sagi – Schwanden (very sure-footed mountain walkers can shorten the stage by descending from the Niederhorn along the exposed Bärenpfad directly into the Justistal); 8¾ hrs. (Walks 47, 48; West);

6. Schwanden – Blueme – Heiligenschwendi – Thun; 4 hrs. (Walk 49; West).

49 From the Stockhorn to the Faulhorn

Nine peaks south of Thunersee and Brienzersee

Oberstocken – Stockhorn – Niesen – Morgenberghorn – Bällehöchst – Sulegg – Geiss – Tuba – Oberberghorn – Faulhorn – Giessbach

Location: Thun (560m) on the train line between Germany and Italy.
Starting point: Oberstocken (691 m); bus No. 3 [300.56] from Thun.
Destination: Giessbach (566m); by boat [3470, 3310] back across Brienzersee and Thunersee; change in Interlaken.
Walking times: in total 45½ hrs. (86 km).
Difference in height: ascent and descent in total both about 8000m.
Grade: one portion of sure-footedness, two portions of fitness and two pinches of route finding; not all sections of the path are marked.
Best season: July to mid-October.
Eating/accommodation: Berghotels and huts; reserve in plenty of time. Berghotels generally full at weekends.
Food: provisions can be bought in Oey, Mülenen and Zweilütschinen/Gündlischwand.
Map: 253 T Gantrisch; 254 T Interlaken.
Alternative: the trains can be included as and when you want.

'The most rewarding viewpoints are to be found on the fringes of the Alps because you can enjoy not only an overview of the middle ranges and the high mountains in all their glory and stature, but also the view of Switzerland's flat country with its lakes, towns, fields and forests, and bordered by the blue Jura, comes together in delightful contrast.' These well-formulated

Views from the Bällehöchst – Morgenberghorn and Niessen on the extreme right.

For waterproofed romantics – path under the Giessbach falls.

sentences can be read in the introduction to the multi-volume history of the highest peaks in Switzerland and their ascents which the Bernese alpine pioneer Gottlieb Studer published under the title '*Über Eis and Schnee*' (On Ice and Snow) in the 19th century. The viewpoints, Niesen, Sulegg, Faulhorn, are named in this book. If we add the neighbouring Stockhorn, Morgenberghorn, Bällehöchst and the three peaks of Schynige Platte which are also border mountains, then we have these nine peaks all together which we can climb in six days and where we can stay overnight if we so wish. Finally we bounce back down in four hours via Brienzersee and Thunersee. In short, this first class walk proves out to be a route with the most wonderful views for ultra-fit romantics.

The six stages (with walk number and guide book volume):
- 1. Oberstocken – Stockhorn; 4½ hrs. (Walk 1; West).
- 2. Stockhorn – Oey – Niesen; 9½ hrs. (Walks 1, 2; West).
- 3. Niesen – Mülenen – Suldgraben – Gasthaus Suld – Brunnihütte (only open at the weekend, otherwise Gasthaus Suld or Rengglipasshütte); 7¾ hrs. (Walks 2, 45; West).
- 4. Brunnihütte – Morgenberghorn – Rengglipass – Untere Innerberg-Hütten – Underberg – Bällehöchst – Sulegg – Suls-Lobhornhütte; 8¾ hrs. (Walks 45; West – 9; East).
- 5. Suls-Lobhornhütte – Isenfluh – Zweilütschinen – Geiss – Schynige Platte; 7 hrs. (Walks 9, 23; East).
- 6. Schynige Platte – Tuba – Oberberghorn – Faulhorn – Giessbach; 8 hrs. (Walks 24, 26; East). Or halve the stage and stay overnight on the Faulhorn.

50 Hintere Gasse from Meiringen to Gsteig

The most beautiful little road in Switzerland – the alpine pass route

Grosse and Kleine Scheidegg – Sefinenfurgge – Hohtürli – Chindbettipass – Ammertenpass – Trütlisbergpass – Chrine

Starting point: Meiringen (595m) on the train line [470] Luzern-Interlaken.
Destination: Gsteig (1184m) on the postbus line [120.15] Gstaad-Les Diablerets. Gstaad lies on the train line Montreux-Oberland-bernois [120].
Walking times: in total 53 hrs. (120 km).
Difference in height: in total about 8800m in ascent; in descent 600m less.
Grade: a good deal of fitness, sure-footedness. Waymarked throughout.
Best season: July to September.
Eating/accommodation: from five-star

hotel as far as the alpine hut.
Food: in the villages on the way (at least every two days).
Map: 254 T Interlaken, 255 T Sustenpass, 263 T Wildstrubel, 264 T Jungfrau; walking maps Berner Oberland Ost and West, 1: 60,000, by Kümmerly+Frey.
Alternatives: peaks that are on the way: Schwarzhorn, Männlichen, Ammertenspitz, Tube, Lauenehorn, Walliser Wispile.
Advice: offered by the Zurich travel agency Eurotrek under the name 'Bärentrek' (℃ 01462 02 03).

'Hintere Gasse' is the name of the Bernese Oberland long distance path on the boundary between the white high Alps and the green pre-Alps. The path from Meiringen to Gsteig is part of the alpine pass trail from Sargans to Montreux which comes from the Rhein valley through the villages of Weisstannen, Elm, Linthal, Altdorf, Engelberg and finally over the Jochpass (compare Walks 44, 45 from volume East) into the Oberland and leaves it at Gstaad over the Col de Jable (→ Walk 11 from volume West) to L'Etivaz and over den Col de Jaman in the direction of Geneva Lake.

The route – also in the Rother walking guides for Bernese Oberland – described below deviates in some places from the usual Hintere Gasse. It chooses, especially between Kandersteg and Lenk, the alternative which is closer to the high mountains across the Engstligenalp instead of the path via Adelboden which is less attractive due to the ski circus on the Hahnenmoos pass. The usual route stops over in the villages, whereas your route frequently prefers mountain inns at a higher altitude. So set off in the morning with the light flooding through the landscape and walk in the evening sun towards the destination of the day.

The eight stages (with walk number and guide book volume):
- ■ 1. Meiringen – Grosse Scheidegg; 5¼ hrs. (Walk 30; East).
- ■ 2. Grosse Scheidegg – Grindelwald – Kleine Scheidegg; 6¼ hrs. (Walks 30, 20; East).
- ■ 3. Kleine Scheidegg – Trümmelbach – Stechelberg – Rostockhütte; 7½ hrs. (Walks 20; Ost – 38; West).
- ■ 4. Rotstockhütte – Sefinenfurgge – Griesalp – Bundalp; 5¾ hrs. (Walks

Close contact with the big mountains – Kleine Scheidegg with the Eiger North Face.

38, 39; West).
- 5. Bundalp – Hohtürli – Kandersteg; 6½ hrs. (Walk 39; West).
- 6. Kandersteg – Schwarenbach – Rote Chume – Chindbettipass – Engstligenalp; 7¾ hrs. (Walks 42, 30; West).
- 7. Engstligenalp – Ammertenspitz – Lenk 6¼ hrs. (Walk 31; West).
- 8. Lenk – Trütlisbergpass – Lauenen – Chrine – Gsteig 8 hrs. (Walks 16, 12; West).

Index

References are to the walk numbers.

GLOSSARY FOR MOUNTAIN WALKERS

German	English	German	English
Alp	alpine meadow, pasture	Hütte	hut
		klein	little
Alphütte	summer dwelling of alpine farmer	Klettergarten	climbing area
		Klettersteig	via ferrata
		Lücke	notch
Bach	stream	Luftseilbahn	cable railway
Bahn	railway	Nord	north
Berg	mountain	Ost	east
Brücke	bridge	Pension	b&b
Fall (pl. Fälle)	waterfall (falls)	Pfad	path
Fluss	river	Sattel	col
Gasthaus	inn, guesthouse	Schlucht	gorge
Gipfel	summit, peak	Schulter	shoulder
Gletscher	glacier	See	lake
Gletscher-schlucht	glacier gorge	Seilbahn	cable railway
		Sesselbahn	chairlift
Gondelbahn	cable car	Süd	south
gross	big	Tal	valley
Höhenpfad	high trail	Weg	path, way, trail